Mindfulness

Mindfulness

Walking with Jesus and Buddha

Sister Annabel Laity

ORBIS BOOKS
Maryknoll, New York 10545

Founded in 1970, Orbis Books endeavors to publish works that enlighten the mind, nourish the spirit, and challenge the conscience. The publishing arm of the Maryknoll Fathers and Brothers, Orbis seeks to explore the global dimensions of the Christian faith and mission, to invite dialogue with diverse cultures and religious traditions, and to serve the cause of reconciliation and peace. The books published reflect the views of their authors and do not represent the official position of the Maryknoll Society. To learn more about Maryknoll and Orbis Books, please visit our website at www.orbisbooks.com

Copyright © 2021 by Plum Village Community of Engaged Buddhism

Illustrations by Regina Gelfer

Published by Orbis Books, Box 302, Maryknoll, NY 10545–0302.

Manufactured in the United States of America

Library of Congress Cataloging-in-Publication Data

Names: Laity, Annabel, author.
Title: Mindfulness : walking with Jesus and Buddha / Sister Annabel Laity.
Description: Maryknoll, NY : Orbis Books, [2021] | Includes bibliographical
    references. | Summary: "Introduction to the principles of mindfulness,
    as taught by Zen master Thich Nhat Hanh, and "double belonging," the
    identification with more than one religious path"—Provided by publisher.
Identifiers: LCCN 2020036325 (print) | LCCN 2020036326 (ebook) |
    ISBN 9781626984158 (trade paperback) | ISBN 9781608338795 (epub)
Subjects: LCSH: Christianity and other religions—Zen Buddhism. | Zen
    Buddhism. | Zen Buddhism—Relations—Christianity. |
Awareness—Religious aspects. | Attention—Religious aspects. |
Mindfulness (Psychology)
Classification: LCC BQ9269.4.C5 L36 2021 (print) | LCC BQ9269.4.C5
    (ebook) | DDC 261.2/43—dc23
LC record available at https://lccn.loc.gov/2020036325
LC ebook record available at https://lccn.loc.gov/2020036326

In Memory of my Father
Reginald Harvey Laity (1918–2017)

Contents

PART II
Double-Belonging

Acknowledgments

I wish to express deep gratitude to my teacher the Venerable Dhyana Master of Plum Village Thich Nhat Hanh without whom I would never have understood and come to practice mindfulness; to my community of practice, who have supported and given me the time and space to write, especially to my monastic brothers and sisters who read the text and offered very useful criticism; and to Robert Ellsberg of Orbis Books for many helpful suggestions.

Introduction

My teacher, the Venerable Thich Nhat Hanh (whom I like to call Thay[1]), is the one who introduced me to the term *double-belonging*. It was during a retreat at Nottingham University, UK, in 2012, with nearly one thousand retreatants present, many, if not most coming from a Christian background. I am always moved by the way Thay introduces Christianity into his talks or writings.

It is not a theoretical or abstract comparison, but rather makes the words of the Bible very concrete, something I can use in my daily practice. He has encouraged me to write a book on Christianity and Buddhism, and see what it is that Christianity can offer to Buddhism. This has helped me to follow in his footprints and discover how to make Christianity a practice for everyday life. The teachings of Jesus in the gospels are like doors that can be opened to find a daily practice of mindfulness. One of the reasons why Thay and I found each other was that he is not caught in Buddhism. Another reason is that he has

---

[1]Thay is the Vietnamese word for teacher.

understood and appreciated the more beautiful aspects of our Western culture.

In our time, many of us have become familiar with the term *double-belonging*. It means you can belong to more than one spiritual tradition. It could be Christianity and Buddhism or Buddhism and Judaism or any other combination of two or more paths. You begin to see Buddhism with Christian eyes or Christianity with Buddhist eyes. You do not have to choose this or that. Christians, while going to church and upholding their Christian practice, can also benefit from mindfulness and meditation retreats led by Buddhist monks and nuns.

I, myself, though a Buddhist nun, am also one who *doubly belongs*. Although well versed in the Buddhist scriptures and meditation practices, I still have in me the religion of my ancestors, my parents, and my childhood. When I go to the church for a funeral service, to support our neighbors, for example, I still make the sign of the cross and genuflect. These things are not outer forms but gestures that help my mind and body to be present in the here and the now. The sign of the cross is made with one in-breath and one out-breath. I listen to the Christian scriptures and recognize the meaning of the words in the light of what I have learned from Buddhism. I often feel deeply moved during these services when I recognize how the roots of the spiritual life transcend the boundaries of separate religions.

I began life as an Anglican and was baptized as a baby in the Anglican Church. I attended a Catholic convent as a primary school child and then as a middle schooler went to a Church of England school. At London University, I attended the Catholic chaplaincy. During my early years, I felt free to go back and forth between the Anglican and Catholic Churches.

The practice of mindfulness, although taught in detail by the Buddha, can fit in with the teaching of any religion or spiritual path. Here, in this book, we want to look at how Christians can make mindfulness a part of their everyday lives.

Sometimes we say that Buddhism is not a religion but an art of living. Practicing a religion, you feel devotion or awe in the presence of God. When you practice mindfulness you still have that sense of awe: when you look up at the night sky and see the galaxies, when you look at the Himalayan or Alpine ranges covered in snow sparkling in the sunlight, when you see a tiny flower poking out of the grass.

Mindfulness helps you to notice the wonders of life because you are not being carried away by thoughts about the past or the future, but it is not a religion.

I learned about mindfulness first from my teacher Thay, who has been called the Father of Mindfulness.[2] I

---

[2] *Time* magazine, January 24, 2019, and the *Irish Times*, April 10, 2012.

also learned from my blood father, Reginald Laity, who taught me how to varnish a boat in mindfulness, without hurrying to finish the job, or how to peel an apple in mindfulness and then eat it in mindfulness.

In the end, everyone has to find their own way. The important thing is to do just that and not be caught in doctrines, theories, or ideologies. Your spiritual path is for you alone, and no two people's paths will be exactly the same. You can make these little teachings on mindfulness part of your spiritual life. They can bring you more happiness, and they may also bring you nearer to the heart of Jesus Christ and Christianity.

What is mindfulness? Mindfulness is the ability to dwell in the present moment, the only moment when life is possible. This will make it possible for us to be aware—to recognize what is happening within ourselves and what is happening around us. Mindfulness helps us to concentrate on what we are doing. We can begin by being aware of our bodily activities of breathing, walking, and eating, for example. Then we can be aware of our feelings and thoughts that, if we are not mindful, can go by unnoticed. Because we are aware of what is happening in the present moment, we can live in the present moment, free from regrets about the past or worries about the future.

Does everyone have the capacity to be mindful? We all have the capacity, but we do not use it. You may remember one time in an emergency situation, you had to be 100 percent there in the present moment and do just what needed to be done. You could not waste any energy thinking about the past or the future. Your capacity for mindfulness at that moment was very important and could have saved your own or someone else's life.

We do not have to wait for an emergency in order to be mindful. If we want, we can use that capacity every day. Breathe in and just recognize you are breathing in. Breathe out and just recognize you are breathing out. Breathe in and switch on the light. Breathe out and take a step away from the light switch. As you switch on the light, be aware of what you are doing. You may repeat a poem to yourself as you put your hand on the light switch to be more aware:

> Forgetfulness is the darkness, (breathe in)
> Mindfulness is the light, (breathe out)
> Awareness comes back, (breathe in)
> And lights up the world. (breathe out)

The practice of mindfulness can be described as setting your feet in a wide-open place.[3] When we practice dwelling in the present moment, we find space in the present

---

[3] See *The New Jerusalem Bible* translation for Psalm 31:8: You "have given me freedom to roam at large."

moment, as we allow our minds to rest there and not be carried away by meaningless thinking. The practice of mindfulness is not a constraint but allows us to feel spaciousness.

One of the teachings of Thay, for which I am most grateful, is the teaching on walking meditation. About ten years ago I was busily walking somewhere on an errand while organizing a retreat in the European Institute of Applied Buddhism in Germany. Thay was walking down the staircase, and I was walking unmindfully up it. When I came close to him, he said, with much love, "Here is your challenge. Every step can bring happiness." Thay has said that if people want one way to find happiness, it is to take every step in mindfulness. If people can do this, it will save the world. This for me is the deepest teaching. Every step, wherever you are and whatever you are doing, can bring happiness. Even if you are going through many difficulties, you can still take a peaceful step and smile. It is a challenge. Can you do it? It is up to you, because happiness does not come from outside. Every day I take up that challenge from my first steps in the early morning until my last steps at night. Thay cannot walk at the moment,[4] but his disciples can walk for him.

Many great spiritual teachers and mystics have been

---

[4] He suffered a severe stroke in 2014.

able to expand the boundaries of their spiritual path and help their spiritual path to grow. If a tree is truly alive, it will send out new branches and leaves every year. The same is true of spiritual paths; they need to renew themselves. All of us have the capacity to help renew our own spiritual path in order to make it more relevant to our own times, able to reduce the suffering of our times and especially the suffering of young people.

The expansion of our spiritual boundaries may begin with intellectual knowledge, but it cannot stay that way. It depends on our daily practices. When we see that a certain daily practice brings about transformation in our life, then we have faith in that practice. That is not blind faith but is based on something concrete.

Our practice of mindfulness leads to a better ability to focus and to concentrate. When we concentrate, we are able to see things more clearly, more as they are, and this helps us expand the boundaries of our spiritual paths.

Once a Vietnamese Catholic nun was visiting our monastery. She had an interview with Thay. She said she was enjoying the practice of Buddhist meditation very much and was wondering whether she should leave her order and become a Buddhist nun. Thay said, "My child, your order really needs you. Please stay with the path you have chosen. You can continue to practice mindfulness as a Christian nun and you can help your order and the world by doing so."

Thay also said, "We do not need people to convert to Buddhism, we have enough Buddhists already. Please go back to your roots and renew them. In the past Christian missionaries came to Vietnam and tried to persuade us to give up our ancestral altars, a very important and meaningful part of the Vietnamese spiritual life. We do not want to do the same kind of thing when we come to the West."

You can do the practices suggested in this book, for instance, mindful breathing, walking, and eating, on your own. However, they become much more enjoyable and easier when you do them with others, either in a retreat setting or in an informal gathering. Throughout the world there are groups practicing mindfulness together, and some Christian churches have their own mindfulness groups.

PART I

Mindfulness

A Way to Happiness

The nineteen chapters in Part 1 are guides to bringing mindfulness into daily life. The day presents us with many opportunities to practice mindfulness. Mindfulness can be creative. Some examples of the author's personal practice are presented here, but you can augment them with your own experience of doing one thing at a time with your true presence in the here and now. This means that you can find different activities in the day into which you want to bring more mindfulness. You can even keep a little notebook. At the end of the day you can look back and see what things you wished you had done more mindfully, and you can write down your aspiration how to practice the next day. For example:

"Today I was irritated with my colleague and unable to look at her. Tomorrow I want to offer her a mindful smile and enquire about her health. In order to do that I shall need to be aware of my breathing and my steps and aware of the presence of God within me and within her."

or:

"Today I walked up and down the stairs several times, but I was not truly present, and my heart was not at peace. Tomorrow I want to enjoy my steps for my own nourishment and peace, not thinking about the past or the future as I walk."

When we have peace in our heart it ripples out from us, into those we live with, work with or simply come into brief contact with during the day. The practice of mindfulness makes us more peaceful people. Please enjoy this practice. It is not meant to be hard work.

1

Breathing Mindfully

He breathed on them and said: "Receive the Holy Spirit."

—JOHN 20:22

The Buddha said that the mindful breath is like a cool breeze on a hot summer's day. Before the rainy season in India, the weather is very hot. Sometimes a cloud will cross over the face of the sun and a cool breeze will come out of the cloud. So, when we take mindful breaths, it takes all the heat out of our thinking and planning.

In the Buddhist tradition I have learned many exercises connected with mindful breathing.[1] The first exercise of mindful breathing is simply to recognize that "This is the

---

[1] *The Anapanasati Sutta*, translated and annotated in Thich Nhat Hanh's *Breathe, You Are Alive: The Sutra on the Full Awareness of Breathing* (Berkeley, CA: Parallax Press, 2008).

in-breath," as it happens, and "This is the out-breath," as it happens. Our minds are wholly focused on recognizing this. The second exercise is to stay with the in-breath for the whole of its length. This means that we are aware of the in-breaths at every millisecond until it turns into our out-breaths and then we are aware of our out-breaths in the same way. The third exercise is to be aware of our whole bodies as we breathe in and out. At this point our breathing has brought our bodies and minds into close contact with each other. The fourth exercise is when the quality of our breathing is able to relax our bodies.

We can breathe the breath of the Buddha and the breath of Jesus, which is holy, the Holy Spirit. It is also the breath of God: "Breathe on me, breath of God." In Buddhism, we practice to let the Buddha breathe. Sometimes we lack confidence in our own abilities to breathe mindfully, so we summon up Jesus, God, or Buddha in us to breathe with and for us. In this way we can let Jesus breathe, we can let God breathe.

When a baby is born, the umbilical cord is cut. The mother no longer breathes for the baby. Babies have to learn to breathe for themselves. After expelling the liquid from its lungs, it can take its first breath. That is a great comfort, the comfort of survival. So, we can also call the breath the Comforter, from that moment on until we die. The Holy Spirit can be understood as mindful breathing that has the quality of holiness. *Spiritus* means breath, and the Holy Spirit is also known as the Comforter or the Helper.

The breath makes our life possible, and the mindful breath enhances our life. Job (27:3) says, "The spirit of God is in my nostrils." Mindful breathing is the gateway to the spiritual life. When you feel you have become enmeshed in the material things of life, you can remind yourself to breathe in and out consciously. The important thing is to give all your attention to your breathing. You do not force your breathing. Rather you enjoy the feeling of your breath in your body. When you want to give your full attention to an object—a rose, your child, or the moon—the best way is to come back to your breathing and follow your breathing as you give your attention to what your child is saying or what the rose is revealing to you. Mindful breathing increases your ability to concentrate on what you are doing and enjoy fully the precious wonders that are available to you in each moment.

It is our mindful breaths that unite our bodies and minds. In our time, it is common for people to experience the state of mind and body being alienated from each other. Especially when we work on the computer, our minds become absorbed in what is appearing on the screen, and we can forget that we have bodies at all. The breath is the bridge between body and mind. When our breathing is peaceful, our bodies and minds also become peaceful.

Job felt the air of his breath in the nostrils, but we can feel the breath in many parts of our bodies. You can try abdominal breathing. Abdomens are like the trunks of our bodies. When we breathe in, our abdomens rise. When we breathe out, they fall. This is because when we breathe in, the lungs expand and the diaphragm is pushed down, causing abdomens to rise. When we breathe out, diaphragms rise as the lungs deflate and so the abdomens fall. Giving careful attention to our abdominal breathing can help us not to stay in our heads.

Thinking can fuel negative emotions that we are having. When we are in the grips of anger, fear, anxiety, despair, or depression, it is important not to think. Our thinking is centered in nerve cells in our brains, which is like the upper branches of our bodies. If we are caught in the whirlwind of strong emotions, the thinking can cause the branches to break. That is why it is important to take refuge in the trunks of our bodies and shift the focus away from our thinking. We just breathe by bringing all our attention into our abdomens to a point four-fingers' breadth below the navel. Many young people have not learned how to do this, and for that reason they suffer so much from negative emotions that they do not want to live anymore. The number of adolescents who commit suicide is still rising. If we are a parent or a teacher we can learn how to handle our own strong emotions with the help of mindful breathing and then hand this on to our children or pupils.

The mindful breathing is also very deep and wonderful. When we breathe mindfully, we recognize that our breathing has a certain quality  that we may or may not be able to describe in words. That quality can nourish and heal us. We can say to ourselves, "Peace, while breathing," which means that our mindful breathing is bringing a quality of peace into our lives. Then we may notice the position of our bodies: sitting, standing, lying, or walking, and because, thanks to our breathing mindfully, we are truly present, we can feel joy while sitting and so on. We can say to ourselves, "Peace while breathing. Joy while lying." It is so pleasant to be lying down or sitting up straight with nowhere to go and nothing to do.

After practicing for a time, you may notice that there is no I who is breathing. The breathing is just happening because of so many causes and conditions, the medulla oblongata of the brain stem, the lungs, the heart within you, and the air all around you. You could say to yourself, "There is only breathing. There is no one breathing." In Christian terms, you could say that the Holy Spirit makes his dwelling place in the one who practices mindful breathing in this deep way. You may feel, "Peace is the breathing. Joy is the lying," because peace is no longer separate from the breathing, and joy is no longer separate from the lying down. You can say these words to yourself to enhance the experience of peaceful breathing.

There was a time when the Desert Father Abba Macarius taught his disciple to say with each breath, "Lord Jesus, have mercy," adding that such a practice is not difficult. We can do this practice in the twenty-first century, right in the midst of our busy lives. The words *Lord Jesus* can accompany the in-breath and the words *have mercy* accompany the out-breath. If our breath is longer, we can say the whole phrase *Lord, have mercy*, as we breathe in, and as we breathe out, the whole phrase, *Christ, have mercy*. Our whole attention is on our breathing and the spirit of the words we are repeating in our hearts. We can remain in this state of concentration whatever we are doing. If we like, we can remain this way for as long as we are awake.

We are not doing very differently from our Buddhist friends who practice saying the name of Amitabha or our Hindu friends who say the name of Rama, as they breathe in and out.

Why are we, throughout the world, breathing and bringing our attention to the object of our devotion? First of all, it is to cut off the unnecessary and useless thinking that goes on in our heads constantly, bringing us anxiety, craving, and aversion. The second advantage is that the object of our contemplation as we breathe in and out is something beautiful, good, and true. This means that our mind is filled with the wholesome energy that helps us speak and act with understanding and compassion. The seventeenth-century Quaker Isaac Penington wrote, "Prayer is the breathing of the child to the father which begat it." For this Quaker, mindful breathing had become prayer, a way to be in touch with God, or what the Quakers call "That of God within you."

2

Walking Mindfully

∾

And did those feet in ancient time
Walk upon England's mountains green
And was the Holy Lamb of God
On England's pleasant pastures seen?[1]
—WILLIAM BLAKE

The poet William Blake wrote these words in the eighteenth century. Of course, now we have a more global outlook than we did then, and we know that it is not only England's mountains that are green or England's pastures that are pleasant. The green hills and the mountains are there in every country of the world for us to walk upon,

---

[1]It may be considered something of a shame that in 1916 this poem by William Blake was put to music and used as a song ("Jerusalem") to rouse patriotic feelings in the midst of a terrible war. This was far from Blake's intention.

still today, when far more destruction has been done to our environment than had been at the dawn of the Industrial Revolution, when Blake was writing. Sometimes we express our outrage at the damage that has been done to our environment and to our Mother Earth. If we had known how to walk with the feet of the Holy Lamb of God on our Mother Earth that damage would not have happened. It may not be too late to start to walk differently on Mother Earth now. Mother Earth is doing her best. There are still green mountains and hills for us to walk on and preserve with our mindful steps.

We are not always aware of this green and pleasant land because we are not really there. We are running into the future with our plans, or we are imprisoned in the past.

Those feet, the feet of Christ, become your feet as you walk with Christ into the present moment. Aware of your in-breath and out-breath, slowly stand up. As you are standing continue to feel your breathing in your body and feel at the same time the contact between the soles of your feet and Mother Earth. Mother Earth is not just matter. She is also spirit. She is a living, breathing being. Aware of your in-breath take one step, two steps, or three steps, starting with your left foot. Aware of your out-breath take one step, two steps, three steps, or more. You do not need to force your lungs to breathe but allow the in-breath and out-breath to accompany as many steps as it needs. Your out-breath may well be longer than your in-breath. Allow your breath to flow naturally. Awareness of your breathing will help you stay with your steps and help your mind not to wander. Awareness of your breathing helps you to be aware of the contact between the soles of your feet and the ground under them.

You can count the number of steps if you like: "One, two, three . . ." and so on, and you can also use words. When you feel that your walking is nourishing you, you can repeat to yourself, "Nourishing, nourishing." When you feel that your walking is healing you, you can repeat, *"healing, healing."* When you feel that by walking mindfully into the present moment you are becoming more stable and more free, you can say to yourself in rhythm with your walking, "More solid, more free." The important thing is to arrive in every step and to feel at home in every step; the feeling and conviction that this is the only place I need to be at this moment.

Charles Wesley wrote, "Closely walk with Thee to heaven." If our walking is into the present moment, we can feel close to Jesus who knew how to walk on Earth so that the Kingdom of Heaven was not somewhere else. We do not have to wait until we die to experience the Kingdom of Heaven.

Luke chapter 17, verses 20–21² record Jesus as saying that the Kingdom of Heaven is not outside of you in some specific place but is within you (*entos humon*). This reading is supported by the Ancient Syriac version of the gospels. Jesus says that you will not find the Kingdom of Heaven by looking here or there. When you find the Kingdom of Heaven within you wherever you walk, you can walk with Jesus. When William Blake wrote the poem above, he may have been in touch with the Kingdom of Heaven within, which manifested outside of him as the green mountains with Christ walking on them. Thay has taught many of us and I have experienced that we can be in touch with the Kingdom of Heaven when we are fully present in the here and now. When we touch the present moment and the wonders of life deeply, we can see and experience that this planet Earth is the Kingdom of Heaven.

The secret is to arrive in the present moment with this very step. If you want to arrive in the future at some future destination, you will be intent on that. Of course, your subconscious mind remembers that you are going

---

²"The coming of the Kingdom of God does not admit of observation and no one can say: *Look it is here, look it is there*. For the kingdom is within you."

to the dining room or the bus stop, but your conscious mind is aware of every step and enjoys every step on the way. Your conscious mind is not caught in thinking about what you will do when you arrive in the dining room. You can be aware of the destination but you are fully present for each step, arriving with each step.

You walk in freedom, as it says in the Psalms: "You have set my feet in a wide, open place."[3] This is about the degree of relaxation and freedom we have as we walk. You are free from regrets about the past and worries about the future, and the whole of eternity is open to you. You walk in a leisurely way because it is relaxed, enjoyable, and brings peace. People sometimes ask whether it is possible to walk mindfully and quickly at the same time. In the beginning you do not automatically walk mindfully. You have a habit of being carried into the future or the past by your thinking as you walk. So, you need to train yourself. As you train yourself, you need to give your full attention to the sensation of the ground under your feet, which is not so easy if you walk quickly.

At first you can train yourself to walk mindfully in a particular place. There must be a stretch that you walk every day of about thirty to fifty meters or less. It may be a flight of stairs. That stretch is your training ground.

---

[3]Psalm 31:8 in the New Jerusalem Bible: "You have given me freedom to roam at large."

Every time that you walk there, you walk being aware of every step. If you forget, you can go back to the beginning. It may be the stretch from your house to the bus stop or from the car park to your office. It may be in the train station or the subway. That place can become the sacred ground for your being in touch with the Earth and the sky. Mother Earth is in you and all around you. You are the Earth, and the Earth is you. You are born from the Earth, and when you die you go back to the Earth. When you feel this close connection to the Earth you will no longer be afraid of death.

If you are a doctor or a psychotherapist you may see many patients in a day, and each one will bring his or her own particular kind of suffering for you to listen to. How can you digest so much suffering? One psychotherapist decided that after seeing a patient, he would accompany him or her to the exit and he would also accompany the next patient from the waiting room to his consulting room. He would always use this time to walk in mindfulness and let go of the suffering and stress of his patients. He also taught them mindful walking.

3

Eating Mindfully

∽

*Jesus took bread and when he had
said the blessing he broke it and gave
it to the disciples. "Take it and eat,"
he said, "this is my body."*

—MATTHEW 26:26

Sometimes I imagine how I should have felt if I had been with the disciples at that time, and I had heard Jesus say the words above. No doubt I should have brought all my attention into the present moment and into eating the bread with all my respect and love for my teacher. This was the last time Jesus was to eat with his disciples before the crucifiction, but it must have been the last of so many times when teacher and disciples ate together. On that Passover night, when Jesus took the bread and broke it, it was not the first time that he had done so. He must have looked deeply into the bread on many occasions in order to see that it was his body. His deep aspiration was that his disciples would feel his energy entering them when they ate mindfully together. As part of the practice of a mindful meal, I invite Jesus to be near, and gently he reminds me to eat today's food and not the food of tomorrow or yesterday.

The teaching of the Eucharist is immensely important for our own time, when the populations of affluent nations are plagued by eating disorders and obesity. Food is seen as some kind of inert matter that we use to gratify our senses, to cover up our anxiety, to make us fat or thin. We have lost the ability to see food as something precious, something filled with spirit. As we cook, we bring our spirit into the food. If we cook with mindfulness, love, and gratitude, the spirit of those positive energies enriches the food. If we cook without mindfulness, in order to finish cooking as quickly as possible and then eat without mindfulness in order to finish eating as quickly as possible, the food loses all of its value. You could say it still has caloric value, but its spiritual value has gone. If, on top of that, as we cook or as we eat, we have thoughts of hatred or anger, the energy of our emotions goes into the food, making it very difficult to digest.

Jesus has shown us by the institution of the Eucharist that eating can be a time of deep meaning that can heal. Participating deeply in a celebration of the Eucharist, we can receive a grace that helps us practice mindful eating for the rest of the week. Whenever we eat, cook, or handle food in any way, we must see that every thought we have over the food will enter the food and make a vessel for healing or for illness. *Eulogein* (the word that is translated as "said the blessing" in the quotation above) can mean to consecrate with prayer or to ask God's blessing on a thing. This means that by our prayerful attitude over the food, we can make it holy. St. Paul, in 1 Corinthians 11:27–30, reminds the disciples of the importance of mindful eating. If we do not eat mindfully, we cannot recognize (*diakrinein*) the body. Here the body must mean the body of Christ. According to Paul if we eat without mindfulness, we can become sick and even die.

A meal is a precious time of togetherness. It is not just the food that we hold in deep awareness but also the presence of those who are eating with us. Statistics show that a family meal at least three times a week does much to increase the chances of stability in the family.[1] We cannot be there for each other when we are watching the television or reading the newspaper as we eat. All members of

---

[1] Frank J. Elger, Wendy Craig, and Stephen J. Trites, "Family Dinners, Communication, and Mental Health in Canadian Adolescents," *Journal of Adolescent Health*, vol. 52, no. 4 (April 2013): 433-38. Benefits include less substance abuse, less behavioral problems, less obesity, better communication skills, etc.

the family can contribute to the preparation of the family meal by helping in the kitchen, making a flower arrangement, or setting the table. At the beginning of the meal, we may hold the hand of the person sitting next to us, so that everyone sitting at the table feels bonded to each other. Someone can say a few words to begin the meal, or we can sing a song of gratitude together.

In Plum Village, the monastery where I live, we sometimes just say, "This is a happy moment" or "I know you are there, and I am very happy." We can also say a few words about the food that we are about to eat, or there can be an expression of gratitude to God or to the elements that have made up the meal, including the cooks. Having a meal together is an opportunity for mindful conversation—to share and to listen to each other—and that is why it is important for the stability and happiness of the family. Some people say that they just do not have the time to enjoy a family meal. Sixty years ago, the average time spent at the dinner table was ninety minutes. Now it is fifteen minutes. It seems we no longer take the time to eat with each other, but we can all organize our lives differently in order to take time to be together so our meal times can be truly meaningful.

In Plum Village, we have a family meal with the whole community of several hundred monks, nuns, and laypeople every Sunday. Everyone serves themselves food, and with our bowls of food, we all walk mindfully to the meditation hall. We wait for everyone to arrive, and then we read our contemplations before eating, which remind us of all the causes and conditions that have brought the food to us. We want to feel grateful, to eat with moderation, and to eat in a way that preserves our health and our planet. We also want to use the energy that we receive from the food to live a wholesome life of love and understanding, and to strengthen our sisterhood and brotherhood. In silence we chew each mouthful at least thirty times in order to practice the contemplations we have read and to make it easier for our bodies to digest the food. The atmosphere of brotherhood and sisterhood, happiness and mindfulness, is very strong, and we can see clearly that to eat with spiritual friends is a wonderful way to nourish not only our bodies but also our minds. We can understand why the early Christians came together to eat a meal and the celebratory nature of eating in the Jewish tradition.

Sometimes we eat because we are hungry, but sometimes we eat when we are not hungry in order to cover up the sorrow or anxiety we may be feeling. One of the best ways to eat only what we need, and what can heal our bodies and minds, is to take care of negative feelings by mindful breathing or walking. As the urge to go to the refrigerator to take something to eat comes up in us, we recognize the unpleasant feelings that we want to cover up and give our attention to calming those feelings. Whenever we eat a snack, we may want to establish a habit of giving thanks for the food with a few breaths before we begin to eat it in mindfulness.

Once we have put a spoonful of food into our mouths, do we really eat it? Do we really taste it? Do we really swallow it? Or does the food become a virtual reality, and what we chew is our thinking more than the food? We do not want to eat our negative thoughts. Visualizing the wheat growing in the field in the rain or sunshine as we eat our pieces of bread can help us be in touch with what we are eating. Gratitude for the food and for those who prepared it is also the positive kind of thinking that keeps us in touch with the food and brings us happiness.

On Sunday or a feast day we may go to a celebration of the Eucharist to receive the body and blood of Christ in the form of bread and wine. As a child I had faith that the priest was giving me the body and blood of Jesus. In my twenties I no longer had that faith. After becoming a Buddhist nun in my late thirties, I wanted to look again at the meaning of the Eucharist. There were times I was in an interfaith gathering and the Catholic priest present would be asked if he would celebrate a Mass for any of the participants who wanted to attend. I watched the priest carefully as he blessed the bread and wine, broke the bread, and handed it to those present. Mindfulness means that every gesture is made with dignity, respect, and loving-kindness.

A day later I watched the priest serving his lunch and it was in the same spirit as he celebrated the Mass.

We can bring mindfulness to our own dinner tables, without being too formal. Christians who eat in mindfulness can feel the presence of God and Christ at every meal. The cosmic Christ, son of the living God, is present in all things. In our refectory in the monastery, we have a calligraphy of Thay that reads, "The bread you hold in your hand is the body of the whole cosmos." When contemplating these words, I feel Buddhism and Christianity and maybe all religions coming together. As a Christian, you could say, "The bread you hold in your hands is the body of the Cosmic Christ." When you are about to put the bread in your mouths, and while you chew it, you see that it contains the whole universe: the sunshine, the rain, and the dust of the stars. Look into the bread and see the grain ripening on the stalk, being nourished by the sunshine and by the rain.[2] See the leaf of a vegetable before it was picked in the garden, the hands that picked it, washed it, and cooked it. You will know that you are not separate from all these things, and you are not alone. The cosmic Christ has no beginning and no end. Once in an ecumenical gathering, I heard a Greek Orthodox priest

---

[2]This meditation is found in the writings of the Franciscan monk Bernabé de Palma (1469–1532) in *Via Spiritus*.

tell a story of when he was in a monastery on Mount Athos. A senior monk came into the kitchen and wept. When asked why, he said, "Monks, you are handling these carrots as if they are inert matter, when in fact they are precious gifts of God containing all the mysteries of the universe. What a waste!"

Saying grace is an expression of gratitude. When we are mindful of all that we receive, we straightaway feel grateful. To feel grateful before we begin a meal or at the end of a meal is good, but to feel grateful as we eat brings us happiness as we eat: grateful to the one who cooked; because we have something to eat, when many will have to go hungry today; and grateful for our family and friends who are eating with us.

A benefit of eating slowly and mindfully is our own health and the health of the planet. Once we have placed the bread or any other food in our mouths, we chew it thirty or even fifty times until the carbohydrates begin to turn into sugar. When we chew the food slowly and carefully, it is much easier to digest, and we recognize when we have eaten enough so that we do not overeat.

Eating mindfully, we are aware of where the food comes from. It is inevitable that some suffering is caused in the production of the food. Even if we claim to be vegan, we can be sure that some little creatures have died in the cultivation of the vegetables we eat. When we are aware of great suffering caused by the eating of certain foods, we will no longer be able to eat them. Awareness of the inhumanity of factory farming will make it difficult for us to eat the meat, drink the milk, and eat the eggs that come from that source. We shall be more careful when we go shopping and look for food that does not cause other species and our planet Earth to suffer so much.

A recent survey[3] shows that mindful eating is necessary if we are to halt the degradation of our planet. The survey states, "Transformation to healthy diets by 2050 will require substantial dietary shifts. Global consumption of fruits, vegetables, nuts and legumes will have to double and consumption of foods such as red meat and sugar will have to be reduced by more than 50%. A diet rich in plant-based food and with fewer animal source food confers both improved health and environmental benefits." In fact, if you eat a diet that is healthy for a human being, that diet is also healthy for our planet. It is wonderful to see how the health of our planet is also the health of human beings in this anthropocene age. Mindful eating will help us change our eating habits into healthy eating habits for ourselves and the whole planet.

---

[3]The Summary Report of the EAT-Lancet Commission on Food, Planet, Health (January 2019).

Sometimes you like to stay just with your chewing, recognizing how your tongue and teeth are moving, keeping out of each other's way. You may recognize that you are eating for your father, mother, and grandparents, keeping them alive in yourself. Eating is to nourish your soul as well as your body. Indeed, this may be what is meant by the words in the Our Father: "Give us today our spiritual bread rather than our daily bread."[4] This reminds us to live our life deeply. At the time of eating, there is nothing to do other than to nourish yourself, your ancestors, and your descendants, so we can give ourselves time to eat in a relaxed way. After eating we do not want to rush away from the table, but rather to sit with our friends and our family and have a nourishing conversation.

---

[4]See Chapter 27.

4

The Bell

⟋

If there is one thing that belongs to global spirituality it is the sound of the bell. Throughout the world, the sound of the bell brings people back to the spiritual dimension.

Once I was standing in our Buddhist nunnery with two Catholic nuns. The monastery bell rang out, and I stopped talking. The two nuns were not surprised at all. They told me that in their convent the bell was rung every hour, and at that time all the nuns would stop what they were doing and recollect that they were in the presence of God.

How in our busy daily life can we have the opportunity to stop running and come back to the present moment? God is always present. It is we who have wandered off somewhere forgetting to be there for God.

When I was a child, the nuns in the convent school

rang the Angelus[1] bell at six in the morning, midday, and six in the evening. The whole school would gather at midday and recite the prayers. Moreover, every class began and ended with prayer. The intention was that the pupils' daily routines would be imbued with spirituality, but too often the prayers became an outer form with no real spiritual content. The secret is to be able to stop running. Our lives are made of a series of events, one leading into another, and often we just want to finish one thing in order to start another. We want to finish washing up in order to have a cup of tea, and then we want to finish the cup of tea in order to turn on the television. We never really stay with what we are doing in order to savor the present moment and be truly alive. If we are not careful, we shall want to finish saying the prayers so we can go and do something different.

The Angelus (Millet, 1859) is a famous painting. Here you see a peasant man and woman, standing in prayer at dusk, in a field where they have been digging potatoes. The painting has the ambience of peace. The peasants have laid aside their tools in order to respond to the sound of the bells and return to the spiritual dimension. When the artist was asked whether he painted the scene out of piety, he replied that he was not religious. It was a

---

[1] The prayers said at these times concern the incarnation of Jesus Christ, and as we pray, we feel the spirit of Jesus Christ being born in our hearts.

scene he remembered from his childhood, a happy childhood memory. While his family was working in the fields and the Angelus bell rang out, his grandmother would remind him to stop what he was doing and pray for the souls of the departed. It was a memory of the spiritual life he treasured.

One time when Thay was in Prague, he heard the Angelus bell. The sound was pure and clear, and he was able to touch the beauty and soul of ancient Europe and many generations. In France and Germany, we practice walking meditation around midday, and when we hear the Angelus bell of the nearby churches, we stop walking and like Thay are in touch with many generations who have listened to that sound. We do not need to think about anything and can be fully present. In France, we sometimes hear the sound of bells coming from three different directions from three churches in the same area. We may either pray in words or silently allow the sound of the bell and the silence of our mind to renew us. Apart from us monks and nuns and the lay practitioners who come and stay with us, I have not seen the villagers stop as they used to do many years ago, but fortunately the bell is still rung. That is a grace. We need bells to remind us to stop and enjoy the fact that we are alive. If not, we could be running all day long until the end of our lives, and then we may regret that we have not allowed ourselves to enjoy the precious moments that life has to offer.

The sound of the bell is an important part of the practice of mindfulness. It helps us stop our body, speech, and thinking from always running into the future or going back into the past. It helps us be truly present, with our body and mind no longer in two different places. The bell says, "Stop, breathe, and enjoy being alive."

In my monastery, we do not talk about "ringing the bell" but we say "invite the bell."   It means invite the bell to sound. The person who invites the bell prepares herself by breathing in and out mindfully before taking the bell in her hands and helping it to sound. He or she recites a short verse and vows to send her  heart of love and compassion along with the sound of the bell, praying that everyone who hears it may awaken from forgetfulness and transcend the path of anxiety and sorrow. The quality of the sound of the bell depends on her peace of mind. If she does not feel peaceful enough, she asks someone else to invite the bell.

Not all of us live near a church or a monastery. So we need ersatz bells. If you work on a computer, the sound of the bell can be downloaded using an app to help you stop and breathe mindfully every half hour or so.[2] Your

---

[2]You may wish to find out more about Mindfulness Apps at https://plumvillage.org/mindfulness-practice/mindful-apps/.

breathing will renew your body and mind. You can close your eyes and give all your attention to your in- and out-breath as you listen to the sound of the bell.

Every time your telephone rings, rather than answer straightaway, you can enjoy one, two, or three in- and out-breaths in order to be in the presence of God before you reply, so that your voice on the phone will be reassuring and kind.

In Buddhism, we say the sound of the bell brings us back to our true home. In Christianity, we say the sound of the bell brings us into the presence of God. There is really no difference between the feeling of being at home in our body and mind and the feeling of being in the presence of God. They are just different words describing the same thing. Our conscious breathing is important to help us stop and be in the presence of God.

After a while whenever you hear a bell you will automatically come back to yourself and be aware of the breath in your body. In order to pray, our mind needs to be very still. So we can begin a session of prayer with the sound of the bell. Conscious breathing helps us still our mind and empty it of unnecessary thinking.

5

The Present Moment

∾

No one can serve two masters; you cannot serve both God and wealth.

That is why I am telling you not to worry about your life and what you are to eat, nor about your body and what you are to wear. Surely life is more than food and the body more than clothing? Look at the birds in the sky. They do not sow or reap or gather into barns: yet your heavenly father feeds them. Can any of you, however much you worry, add one cubit to your span of life? And why worry about clothing? Think of the flowers growing in the fields: they

> *never have to work or spin. Yet I*
> *assure you that not even Solomon in*
> *all his royal robes was clothed like*
> *one of these. Set your hearts on your*
> *heavenly father's kingdom first and*
> *all these other things will be given to*
> *you as well. So do not worry about*
> *tomorrow: tomorrow will take care*
> *of itself.*
>
> —MATTHEW 6:24–34

My father's favorite part of the gospel has become mine as well. When I was a child, I often heard my father quote these verses. Why do we not allow the future to take care of itself? Why do we worry about so many unnecessary things, which we have no power to do anything about? Anxiety is like a disease that affects so many people in our own time.

Sometimes we worry about money and our career more than we need to, and we overwork either to cover up the loneliness inside us or to have the security of much more money than we need. Someone taking care of terminally ill people in a hospice would ask her patients if there was anything they regretted and there were five answers that she heard most frequently: (1) I did not allow myself to be happy; (2) I worked too much; (3) I did not have enough time for family and friends; (4) I did not share the deepest things in my heart; (5) I did not do what I wanted to do.[1]

This means that we worry about not having enough money, we work too hard, and we sacrifice the things that are most meaningful in our lives. From time to time we can ask ourselves, "What do I really want to do?" We can look deeply into our hearts and find the answer from our instinctive wisdom. The answer could be, "I want to help the poor, the disadvantaged. I want to have time to be with nature. I want time to be with my loved ones. I want to take care of nature. I want to help young people foster the changes our societies need in order to solve the climate crisis. I want to taste true happiness every day." When we know our deepest desires and allow ourselves to actualize them, we can enjoy fulfillment.

Jesus had time to be with nature, to look at the flowers and enjoy their beauty. This passage is a chance for us to practice the mindfulness of consumption that will help conserve our planet Earth. Consuming unmindfully, we exploit the resources of the Earth and threaten the very continuation of life on Earth. To be content with what we have and to see that we already have enough is the way to be happy ourselves and to help life on this Earth continue for a long time.

---

[1]Bronnie Ware, *The Top Five Regrets of the Dying: A Life Transformed by the Dearly Departing* (Carlsbad, CA: Hay House, 2019).

"Set your hearts on your heavenly father's kingdom first and all these other things will be given to you as well" (Matthew 6:33). This is a deep teaching about our ultimate concern: our understanding of the nature of life, the nature of birth and death, the nature of God and creation. So, we can be mindful of what is most important to us and not lose ourselves in our daily concerns: making money, promotion, loss, gain, praise, and blame.

The Kingdom of Heaven is *entos umōn*, within you. So, setting your heart on the Kingdom is not a search outside of yourself but a journey within. Jesus says, "it is like a seed that can grow into a tree and the birds can come there to nest" (Matthew 13:31). A seed can mean a potential that lies in the deepest levels of our consciousness. The Kingdom is a potential within you, and if it receives the right nourishment, it will grow into a tree and manifest as a wonderful reality in your daily life. You do not have to wait until you die to enter the Kingdom. In fact you need to be very alive. Do you remember a time when you had to sit in a stuffy room in a long meeting? When it was all over, you went out into the garden and breathed in a lungful of fresh air. It was as if you were in paradise. The Kingdom of Heaven was there waiting for you and is always there waiting for you, which is what is meant by the Kingdom of Heaven is at hand.[2] As you

---

[2]See Chapter 27.

walk through a garden of summer flowers or on a hill with little spring flowers peeking out of the grass, if that is not the Kingdom of Heaven, then what is?

We have a tendency to think that there must be somewhere better than this planet Earth. Many astronauts have needed to go up into space in a spaceship in order to recognize that Planet Earth is home. Those of us down here on Earth do not feel it is our home. We are always thinking there must be somewhere better.

The Buddha teaches the same thing in a somewhat different way:

> Do not pursue the past.
> Do not lose yourself in the future.
> The past no longer is.
> The future has not yet come.
> Looking deeply at life as it is
> in the very here and now,
> the practitioner dwells
> in stability and freedom.[3]

This kind of living in the present moment is called living alone by the Buddha. To live alone does not literally mean to live on your own and not to be in company with

---

[3] *Bhaddekaratta Sutta*, Majjhima Nikaya 131.

others. It means to be centered and focused on what one is doing; to be free of the past and the future. If you are sitting listening deeply to someone sharing their difficulties so that you feel there is no longer any barrier between you and him, then the Buddha would say you are living alone, wholly focused on what is happening here and now. If, on the other hand, while you are listening, you listen with only one ear and your mind is wondering what you are going to do next, then you are not living alone; you are living in company with the future.

Many of us suffer from loneliness. You could say it is a sickness of our times. We have made a society where people feel lonely. Being alone in the sense of living deeply in the present moment, without being accompanied by regrets about the past or worries about the future, can be a cure for loneliness. Of course, we need intimacy, we need spiritual friends, but there are times when we need to be alone, either out of choice or because of circumstances. When we are on our own, we can practice mindful breathing in order to be fully in the present moment, and we feel interconnected with everything with which we come into contact. This is what cures the feeling of loneliness.

6

Reconciliation

☙

If you are offering your gift at the altar and remember that your brother or sister has something against you, leave your gift there in front of the altar. First go and be reconciled with them. Then come back and offer your gift.

—MATTHEW 5:23

It is only normal to have a falling out with other human beings, especially those we are close to, but it is also necessary to practice reconciliation. We are all different. No one perceives the world in exactly the same way as anyone else, and because we perceive the world differently, we have falling outs with each other. We have notions and ideas about ourselves and about other people, and they are not correct. Based on these notions and ideas, we give rise to rancor and feelings of ill will. I, for example, may have an idea that you want to hurt or destroy me or my culture or my people. Then, when you do or say something that reinforces the idea I have, I am angry.

At the root of anger lies fear—the fear that you are going to destroy me. That fear is also at the root of terrorism. So we should take care of our little angers and upsets. If we know we have said or done something that could hurt someone, we need to come to them and apologize as soon as we can. You may tell yourself that it was only a little thing and you do not need to make an issue out of it, but the other person could be suffering deeply because of what you said, and your sincere apology will dissolve their suffering. Sometimes when we make a joke, we do not mean to hurt the other person, but the joke is at that person's expense. As soon as we realize that it was an unskillful joke that could be taken as an insult, we should apologize right away.

In the time of Jesus Christ, there was no telephone or e-mail, so you had to go and find the person to apologize; but now we have these means of communication and we can use them to connect with the other person in as short a time as possible: "This morning I said . . . I realize it was very unskillful. Please accept my sincere apology and my intention not to make that kind of remark to anyone in the future."

You will feel much better after saying or writing these words. A sincere apology is an unconditional apology. You do not apologize because you are expecting the other person to apologize in return. You do not need to make excuses for the thing you said. It is clear and simple: "I should not have said that, and I do not want to say things like that ever again."

If someone else apologizes to us, however inadequate the apology may seem, we should accept it: "Forgive us our trespasses as we forgive those who trespass against us." The fact that the others have taken the trouble to apologize shows that they are still willing to communicate. On the level of everyday communication, we accept the apology of the other, even though on a deeper level we are not yet able to forgive. We cannot force ourselves to forgive or forgive with our intellect alone. Forgiveness comes naturally when we understand the suffering and the ignorance of the person we need to forgive, and it may take time to do this. When I feel hurt by the words or actions of another person, I take it as an opportunity to look deeply.

In a conflict, resolution is of three kinds, which we can roughly call unilateral reconciliation, bilateral reconciliation, and both unilateral and bilateral reconciliation. We always begin with unilateral reconciliation; this means we come back to ourselves, with mindful breathing, and we look deeply into ourselves and into the people who have made us suffer. We can do this with the help of a pen and paper if we like, noting down the things we see as we see them. We can look at the physical health, the psychological health, and the spiritual health of ourselves and of the others. We realize that nobody wants to cause suffering. Maybe another person's suffering spills out in unskillful ways. We look deeply, until we no longer feel rancor or resentment, but rather acceptance.

Bilateral reconciliation happens when others agree to share with us and we are able to listen deeply. Listening deeply is an art that takes time to train in and to learn. A Benedictine Father shared in an ecumenical retreat that,

when listening to another person, he allowed himself to be an empty container. He was able to empty himself of all ideas of being a separate self. When we do that, it is easy for the other person to share. Our eyes and our facial expressions reveal acceptance and openness. On the other hand, if we are full of our ideas about ourselves and the others, our presence will put up a wall between us and the others will not be able to share.

If others share things we want to hear, it will be easy to listen. If they share in a negative way, especially pointing out the difficulties they have with us, it is not so easy. We need to remind ourselves that "This person suffers and thinks her suffering is caused by me. I am sitting and listening to help her to suffer less. If I make myself a wall, it will spoil everything." We can learn so much about others if we are able to listen in such a way that we can hear not only what they are saying but also what they leave unsaid. Words are like metaphors. They can never express everything we want to say. It takes deep listening to understand what lies behind the words we hear. Sometimes when I listen deeply to someone, I hear her say I have said or done something, and my first thought is that I have not said or done that. On deeper reflection, I realize that I have an attitude or manner that she could have interpreted in this way. For instance, maybe she feels ignored by me, and listening deeply I realize that I need to change that attitude rather than think I never said that, I never did that.

Before we agree to sit and listen deeply to others, we should be confident that we can keep our compassion alive throughout our listening. If it happens that as we listen, compassion in us dries up, we should gently and politely thank the others for sharing and ask to be able to continue the listening session at another time. There is no point in continuing if we feel anger or resentment. We have to wait until another day.

It is not only our apologies for our mistakes that we need to express. It is also very important to let the other people know how much we appreciate them. Say you are sitting in your car driving, and alongside you is your partner of many years. You forget about that person's presence as you are wholly immersed in your plans for the future. If you could be mindful of the presence of the person sitting alongside you, would that not be a wonderful gift? You would say, "I know you are there and it makes me very happy." These words will make that person's day. The person might have thought that his or her presence in life was not beneficial for anyone and now, hearing your words, the person's *joie de vivre* is reawakened. To be mindful means to present in the here and now for the one who is with us.

A very busy businessman looked in his diary and saw that tomorrow was his son's birthday. He went to his son and asked, "Son, what can I buy you for your birthday present this year?" His son could not think of anything. His family was not poor, and he had all the material things he could want. Finally, the son said he could not think of anything, and the father said to keep thinking and when he had an idea to let the father know. A few hours later the son came back, "Daddy, I know what I want for my birthday. I want you." His father was so busy earning money that he did not have time to spend with his son: to play basketball, to go bicycling, to spend time together sharing joys and disappointments; all these things would bring a great deal of happiness to the son.

Sometimes we have been estranged from someone for a long time. We may have made efforts to contact that person but he is not ready to respond. We need to be patient. Patience is a mark of true love. There are three kinds of action: body, mind, and speech. Mind is the basis of speech and bodily action. So, the first step in reconciliation is taken with our minds. We want to understand that person from whom we are estranged. How does the person suffer? Once we have understood his suffering, we shall be able to feel compassion for him. Even before we understand him, we need to understand ourselves. How have we suffered? What do we want for ourselves? We want to be truly happy. If we want to be happy, that must be true of the other person also, but first we have to feel how much we want to be happy, how much we do not want to suffer. Think about the other person in wishing all positive things for him. We can make this part of our daily meditations or prayers:

> May I be happy, peaceful, and light in
> body and spirit.
> May you be happy, peaceful, and light
> in body and in spirit.

When you feel that you have compassion for the other person you can write a letter in which you recount all the positive things you enjoyed together in the past and express your appreciation for his presence in your life.

When we live together or have frequent contact with

other people, habitual patterns of behavior may arise. We may become irritated by things the other people say. We try very hard not to express our irritation but still it comes out in our reactions. We can sit down with pen and paper and answer some questions for ourselves:

1. What precisely does she do that annoys me?
2. How do I generally react out of this annoyance?
3. What effect on her does my reaction have?
4. Can I react differently?
5. What form would my reacting differently take?

If you love someone, you want to share everything with that person, but you need to share skillfully and find the right time to do so. When you are both relaxed and have plenty of time to be with each other, it is a good moment to share. You can sit down together with a cup of tea. The opening of the conversation is always a deep appreciation of the other person. You can prepare to do this by taking the time to reflect and write down a few things you sincerely like and appreciate about the other person—your partner, colleague, or friend. You give concrete examples of what the other person has said and done for you to show that you are sincere in your appreciation. This will help balance your perception and emotions concerning the other person and water the good seeds in that person.

The next step can be a humble admission of your own shortcomings. After that you can gently introduce the topic of your irritation, for example, "These past few days I have been looking into my irritation. I see that it is something I need to transform for my benefit and for yours. I want to take responsibility for my being irritated with you, and I should also like to ask for your help. I do not know why but when you say/do . . . I feel irritated. I am determined to breathe and take care of my irritation, and I know that by sharing and acknowledging it with you, it will help me to take better care of my emotions. Would it be all right with you if I were to make a sign to let you know I am irritated (like lifting my hand very gently)?"

In your family do you have time to sit together and express appreciation for each other? In our family retreats in Plum Village the most moving part is when the children and parents are able to sit together and share. Mothering Sunday, Mother's Day, or Father's Day could be a good time to start this tradition of sitting together to share. Many families practice this sharing once a week or every month and feel very nourished by it. Before they sit together the children and parents have had time to find a little gift from nature. They do not buy something for each other but find a stone, a leaf, or a flower in nature and make a card with their hands in which they express their appreciation and love—children for parents and parents for children. They practice listening deeply to each other as they share all that is in their hearts as far as appreciating each other is concerned. Often tears of joy are shed because the family members are so moved.

This sharing is also a time for hugging in mindfulness. There is an art to hugging, which makes the hug a very deep experience for children and parents alike. We always ask first: "May I give you a hug?" If there is assent, we give all our attention as we take the other person in our arms. If it is a small child, we may need to sit on our knees to hug them comfortably. We do not need to pat the other people on the backs or squeeze them too tightly. We follow our in-breath and out-breath deeply at least three times. We do not need to think about anything. We just enjoy the moment of feeling our loved ones alive in our arms—the miracle of being alive. We are warm and alive in this moment and so are they. This is a sacred and precious moment.

7

Communion
and
Prayer

∾

If two of you agree to ask for some-
thing, it will be done by my Father
in heaven. For where two or three
gather in my name, I am there with
them.

—MATTHEW 18:19–20

The nineteenth and twentieth centuries were the age of individualism. As a human species we are beginning in the twenty-first century to see again the value of community. Many of us have seen the sacredness of communion, brotherhood, and sisterhood. In all our nonviolent struggles, we take refuge in brotherhood and sisterhood in order to achieve our goals. Those of us who struggle to preserve the beauty of our planet Earth and life upon planet Earth can only do so as a community. That is why we need to be more than one when we pray for something. The spiritual energy of one plus one is more than two. It could be ten times that amount, and if there are hundreds united in spirituality, the energy we produce is a thousand-fold. "In the name of Jesus" means that even though Jesus lived more than two thousand years ago, we can feel his presence, and we can talk to him in this very moment.

Once we have found our spiritual path, we know that we need spiritual friends. They could be Friends at a Quaker Meeting, friends with whom we worship in the church, and so on. It is very difficult to maintain a spiritual practice without the support of friends practicing with us. Friends can guide each other and support each other when one of them is going through a difficult time. We do not just meditate or worship together, we drink tea together, eat a meal together, and sit together as we share about how our lives and spiritual practices are going.

St. Benedict in the Rule[1] talks about different kinds of monks. His conclusion is that the monk who is most likely to be successful in his vocation is, in general, the

---

[1] *The Rule of St. Benedict.* Chapter 1: Concerning the different kinds of monks.

coenobite.[2] We may also find that our family members or our colleagues can be our spiritual community. If our workplace is to become a spiritual community, there should be a number of us who are committed to doing spiritual practice at work. There are hospitals, schools, and even businesses in Asia, Europe, and America where there are a number of people who agree that they will practice together during the workday. At lunch time they can eat mindfully together, starting with a few minutes of eating in silence. After lunch one of them can lead total relaxation for the others.

In many spiritual traditions, people pray together as a community. In the theistic traditions, we may pray for those who are sick or dying, entrusting the person who is the object of our prayer to the care of God. When those who are gathered together focus their attention on a single object of their prayer, a collective energy is produced that can reach the person being prayed for. In Plum Village we say that this is the energy of mindfulness, concentration, and compassion being generated by our mindful breathing and our mind of love. Although there is ample evidence that prayer is effective, it is not possible to explain scientifically how it works exactly. Several cases have been

---

[2] The word comes from the Greek *koinon* (community) and *bios* (life)—those who live in community. Saint Benedict adds that those who practice prayer alone in the desert successfully are very rare exceptions.

reported to our community of the efficacy of our prayers. For example, at exactly the time the prayer is said and the name of the person is read, someone sitting at the bedside of the person being prayed for (though hundreds of miles away) will notice a change in the patient. Someone who is dying becomes peaceful and is able to let go, or someone who is in pain experiences relief.

There must be many causes and conditions that make it possible for the energy of our prayers to reach someone. Mechanically repeating words of prayer without our full attention cannot be sufficient. We need to come back to the present moment and open our hearts to the suffering in other people. Then the energy of concentration and compassion is born, and this can be very powerful and healing.

In prayer there are three elements: the one who prays, the one who is prayed to, and the one who is prayed for. In the beginning of our prayers, we see these three elements as separate, but as our prayers deepen, they become one.

The one who prays needs to be calm and clear enough in order to ask for help, and the prayer must be wholehearted. You pray not just with words but with your whole person, body as well as heart and mind, so the position of your body is important. You can kneel, sit, or stand but your body should be straight so that your mind remains alert. Joining your palms helps you concentrate;

bringing the left side and the right side of your body and brain together. The prostrate position also helps you to pray or make a deep aspiration. In this position your brain and heart are on the same level, and you can easily let go of your preferences and attachments.

Then there is the one who is prayed to. You may pray to God, to a saint, or to someone you consider to be saintly, and in the beginning, you feel sure that being is outside of you. That being is full of wisdom and compassion. As you continue to pray, you feel that wisdom and compassion in your own mind, so you and the being are becoming one.

Finally, there is the one you are praying for. If that person is known to you personally, you may feel within the person the energy of the one you are praying to, as you are feeling it within yourself. Then there is no longer any separation. If the person is not known to you personally, you do your best to visualize the person's circumstances. If you know someone who is closely connected to the person, you can visualize that person as you pray.

As well as praying for others, we can pray for ourselves and for the situation in the world. We can pray for war or natural disasters to end. When we pray in this way, it is much more than asking a favor of God. We feel the energy of God within ourselves, vowing not to say or do things that will lead to conflict or aggravate the climate crisis.

In Christianity there are four kinds of prayer: compunction, vow, sending energy, and gratitude. They are all expressions of mindfulness. Compunction is the prayer we offer when we recognize our shortcomings: the tears we shed when we realize the harm we have done as an individual, a family, a race, or as a human. Our vows are made when we see clearly our way ahead and we commit ourselves to go on that path. *Imprecatio* is praying for others, we could call it sending the energy of our compassion to those who suffer. Gratitude is our expression of joy for all that we have received.

8

Mindfulness of Eternity

∽

And see, I am always with you even
to the end of time.
— MATTHEW 2:19

To see a world in a grain of sand
And heaven in a wild flower
Hold infinity in the palm of your hand
And eternity in an hour.
—WILLIAM BLAKE, 1757–1827

Mindfulness helps us concentrate, and with concentration we are able to reflect and look deeply. Our lifestyles may deprive us of the opportunity to look deeply. If we want, we can always reorganize our busy lives so that we have time for reflection. Generally, the early morning at dawn is the time when our mind is fresh and ready for re-flection. In the evening when the wind dies and shadows start to cross the sky as the sun sets is also a time when the mind naturally becomes peaceful. If our minds are not peaceful and at ease, reflection is not successful and does not lead to insight.

At times, our mind naturally falls into quietude. At other times, we can use our body and breathing to help our mind be at ease. The position of our bodies, upright and relaxed, or even lying down in times of ill health, helps our minds. Our quiet breathing also helps. It is not possible to force our breathing to be gentle and even. This is something that happens naturally when we shine the light of awareness on it. At first, we may be aware that our breathing is hurried and uneven, but as we continue to sit peacefully and be aware of it, it naturally becomes peaceful and calm.

We may want to look deeply into our birth and death. We can ask questions like "When was I born? Was I really born on the day it mentions on my birth certificate? Was I there before my date of birth? Was I there in my mother, father, grandmothers, and grandfathers? When I die shall I continue in my children and grandchildren?" We do not have to answer these questions. They just open up another way of looking. George Herbert expresses looking deeply like someone who is able to look through the glass and see the vista beyond: "A man that looks on glass / on it may stay his eye / or if he pleaseth through it pass / and then the heaven espy."[1]

Mysticism is being in touch with a dimension of life that is normally hidden from intellectual knowledge and everyday patterns of thought. In Christianity, there is a long tradition of mysticism. "The peace of God that is beyond our understanding,"(Philippians 4:7) means the peace that we cannot express in words or concepts or grasp intellectually. It is the peace of the ultimate dimension, the peace of God. If we are able to touch the ultimate dimension by living deeply in the present moment, then this energy of peace and mindfulness will guard our hearts and our thoughts and protect us.

Time is measured by our brains. There is a dimension beyond time and space, which Jesus called "the end of time," where we can always find him. Death is an idea in our minds that we impose upon reality. We have the idea that before his birth someone does not exist, and after his death he goes back into nonexistence. In the Christian church, we talk about *eternal life*. According to the mystical way of looking as expressed by Blake in the quotation above, eternity means another dimension that lies outside of our usual concept of time.

About twenty years ago, while leading Buddhist retreats

---

[1]From "The Elixir" by George Herbert (1633).

in Israel, I was taken to visit the Church of the Holy Sepulchre in Jerusalem. Tired of the crowds, I withdrew to a part of the church that had been abandoned, and there I saw an image of Jesus in my mind, robust, full of life and laughing. I had never imagined Jesus laughing. Maybe he laughed because the different Christian churches could not unite in order to worship together but had to divide the Church of the Holy Sepulchre into different sections. Jesus had escaped all of that and had come here to this grimy, neglected part of the building.

Life has more than one dimension for us to respond to. There is a process of growing up, education, earning a living, raising a family, aging, and dying. During that process we have many everyday concerns, and our whole life can be taken up by that dimension as we run from one activity to the next and one thought to another. This is the historical or conventional dimension of reality. However, it is possible to stop running and to touch another dimension, which we can call the ultimate. There, we can touch the ending of time, the experience that Blake describes as "eternity in an hour." We can understand how it is possible for Jesus to say, "The world will see me no more but you will see me. You will realize that I am in my Father and you are in me and I am in you" (John 14:19).

Although we may not think about it often, there will be a time when we are physically separated from the people we love the most by death. After we have given ourselves the time to grieve, there comes a period of reflection when we feel again the presence of our loved ones. Like a game of hide and seek, we find our loved one where we did not expect to: in ourselves, in other people, in our consciousnesses. More than two thousand years after his death, we find Jesus is walking with us, talking to us today.

We learn to see ourselves clearly in our loved ones: mother, father, children, and partner; in our spiritual teachers and students. We see ourselves and our loved ones as waves on the surface of the great ocean. Thay shared with us that we are at the same time the wave and the water. The wave might enjoy going up and be afraid of going down and dying. But when we realize the insight that our essence is water, then we no longer have fear of dying. The wave represents the historical dimension, and the water represents the ultimate, or God. When the wave breaks on the shore, nothing is lost. The water goes back to the water. The energy continues by turning stones into sand or in the thud that is felt under our  feet as we stand on the shore. When we or our loved ones die, nothing is lost. We just cease to manifest in our familiar forms. This is something scientific: the first law of thermodynamics. In the words of Lavoisier, the eighteenth-century French Father of Chemistry: *"Rien ne se crée. Rien ne se perd. Tout se transforme"* (Nothing is born. Nothing is lost. Everything is in a process of transformation).

The two dimensions of life, historical and ultimate, have a parallel in science. The particle physicist has to recognize the absurdity of the subatomic world, which does not conform to the rules of time and space of the visible world. Newtonian physics still makes sense in the world of large objects, but the world of subatomic particles operates in a different way. The waves on the ocean rise and fall, begin and end, but the ocean water does not conform to the rules of the waves.

9

Mindfulness of Mistakes

☙

*Father, I have sinned against heaven
and against you and am no more
worthy to be called your son. Let me
be one of your hired servants.*
— LUKE 15:18

In the parable of the Prodigal Son, the runaway son
needs to feel regret in order to find his way out of his
miserable situation. We can practice the mindfulness
of deeds we have done that have caused ourselves and/
or others to suffer: mindfulness of regret. Regret can be
positive, or it can be negative. It is important to know
when we have made a mistake and to make the determination not to do the same thing again. If we do that, we
know we have done our best and can let go of all feelings

of shame or guilt. On the other hand, if our regret for a mistake we have made gnaws at us day and night, it is harmful for ourselves and others, and we need to do the practice of repentance.

After repentance, our hearts are light like the clouds that float over the ancient forest. All of us make mistakes. None of us want to do harm. Our mistakes come from our unskillfulness and our ignorance. Sometimes we regret something as soon as we have said or done it. Sometimes we only regret when we see the effect that our actions had on ourselves and the world.

The practice of repentance is, above all, the ability to see that we have done something unskillful and to admit that to ourselves and others, if need be. It is, secondly, the determination not to do this thing again. It can be helpful to share this determination with others so that we feel their support.

The first thing is to forgive ourselves. There is a simple exercise of contemplation that can help one to forgive oneself. First of all, we come back to ourselves with our breathing. Then we recall the action of body or speech that we committed that caused suffering to ourselves and to others. We continue to follow our breathing. We are very clear that in the past we caused that suffering. Then we contemplate the circumstances under which we did that act or said those words. We see how we were not mindful; we were ignorant of the consequences of our action; and we were suffering, maybe, and were trying to find a way out of our suffering. Sometimes we see that we have a tendency to act or speak in certain ways that are very deep in our consciousness. We recognize that this tendency to act unhealthily may have been handed down to us from previous generations. Thanks to our practice of mindfulness, we are able to look deeply into it and transform it over time, so we do not need to hand it on to future generations.

There was an eleven-year-old young man who used to come to mindfulness retreats. His father, like his grandfather before him, was Confucian, and believed that a child should be beaten when he fell down. The son, on the other hand, had a Western education, and believed that a child who fell down should be comforted and taken care of. He was not happy when he fell down and his father manifested anger. He vowed to himself that when he grew up and had his own children, he would never beat them. One day during a retreat, he was watching his little sister playing with another girl in a hammock. The two girls accidentally tipped the hammock over, throwing them onto the ground. His little sister's forehead was bleeding. As he watched the scene, he felt strong feelings of anger rising in him. He wanted to shout at his sister and tell her how stupid she was. However, he was able to breathe deeply and run away from the scene. When he reached the forest, he sat down and realized that he had the same tendency as his father to get angry. At the same time, he realized that his father was angry because his grandfather had been like that, and he could forgive his father. This is quite a remarkable insight for an eleven-year-old boy.

We also see how the wounds of our wrongdoings in the past still lie deep in our consciousness. Seeing all this, we feel compassion for ourselves. Then we say with all our heart as we breathe in, "I am sorry," and as we breathe out, we promise, "I do not want to ever do that again." With this very act of contemplation, we forgive ourselves. After that, we are more in a position to forgive others. We see that they too were unmindful and ignorant as they did or said something to hurt us, that they were suffering and they continue to suffer because of that act. We feel compassion for them and no more rancor.

In our experience we have seen clearly that mistakes or wrongdoing can be healed. Christianity talks about the "forgiveness of sins." I remember asking a priest once, "Why do we have to say mea culpa, *mea culpa, mea maxima culpa*? I cannot see that I have done anything very bad." The priest said that we should not be caught in the word *mea* (my). We want forgiveness for the mistakes of our whole ancestral line, the wrongdoings of our country and people and also for the human species. This could include those who we feel are destroying our environment or are engaged in acts of violence, not because we condone what they are doing but because we see how they suffer because of their ignorance and wrong perceptions. And we ask for forgiveness, because we, too, would suffer if we point the finger and judge them, instead of giving rise to understanding and compassion in our hearts. If we are able to forgive ourselves and others, then the actions and words of the past will no longer have the power to burden us, and we can live more freely and happily in the present moment. We remember the sayings of Jesus about not throwing a stone, if you have ever done something wrong and "take the log out of your own eye first" (Luke 6:41–42). "Do not judge, and you will not be judged. Do not condemn,  and you will not be condemned. Forgive, and you will be forgiven" (Luke 6:37–38).

There is a practice of repentance that we call "touching the earth." It means that while letting go of our mistakes, we touch the ground with most of our body. This position is known to those who practice hatha yoga as the "child pose," when our shins, knees, arms, and forehead are all on the ground.

In the Russian Orthodox Church, I have watched practitioners prostrating like this before the statues of the saints, and Islam also has this practice. The "touching the earth" position is something universal to our human species. Our bodies feel very comfortable in this position of being close to the earth. It puts our hearts and our brains more or less on the same level. Our blood circulates well in our intestines (our second brain, as it is sometimes called). Our mind also feels relaxed and ready to let go of ideas and habit energies. In this position we can make deep aspirations to begin anew, letting go of all that is past and beginning to do differently in the present.

When I am in the touching the earth position, I recognize how closely I am connected to my ancestors; I feel their compassion, generosity, and wisdom running in my veins. At the same time, I am also in touch with their cruelty and their ignorance, and I ask the earth to receive all that and transform it into flowers. I see how I also have the tendency to be cruel, and the earth helps me by allowing me to let go of that tendency. The earth, just as God the Father who is kind to the ungrateful and the wicked, has a wonderful capacity to receive, to forgive and transform. The earth does not become angry when we throw urine or excrement on her; she receives it and transforms it into fruits and flowers.

10

Mindfulness and Celebration

∽

It is only right that we should celebrate and rejoice.

—LUKE 15:51

For the past thirty-five years, I have lived in a community that is not Christian, but we always celebrate Christmas and Easter. They are such important features of the cycle of each year. We also celebrate the nativity of the Buddha and the coming of the New Year. These celebrations enrich our lives and make them more beautiful. They are an opportunity for us to be with our friends and relations in a meaningful way. We can resist the commercialization of Christmas by the way we celebrate.

Celebrations, such as Christmas and Easter, have an outer form that symbolizes an inner content. When I was an adolescent, I began to see a dichotomy between the outer forms of celebration and the inner content of peace and love that the birth of Christ symbolizes. Later on, I realized that this dichotomy does not need to exist. We can give gifts and eat meals in such a way that complements but does not oppose the moments spent in prayer. When we celebrate Christmas, it is because we want Christ to be born in our hearts. One of my favorite practices at Christmastime is to sit or kneel in front of the crib, to come back to my breathing, and to pray for the Christ child to be born in my own and in the hearts of all people.

When I lived in Greece, I learned that for Greek people, Easter is a much more important feast than Christmas. It must be the darkness that we experience in Northern Europe that makes Christmas so important for us. The light has to come from our own hearts. Lighting a candle in mindfulness, we can visualize that we are bringing the light of peace and understanding into the world.

Any celebration is preceded by a period of preparation, which is no less important than the celebration itself. We cook and do other preparations in mindfulness. It is not our aim to celebrate in the future. We celebrate with joy all the way along.

Writing Christmas cards is a wonderful practice. Every

card we write is an opportunity for mindful communication. We may have a list of those we wish to send a card to. We bring into our awareness the person to whom we are addressing this card. Then we contemplate what words would be most appropriate to address to that person. Still bearing the receiver in mind, we write mindfully with love and understanding what we feel is a suitable communication. Mindfully, we put the card in the envelope and seal it with care. We are not just sending paper and ink but the spiritual energy of understanding and love.

Maybe we can buy less at Christmas. We can practice mindful shopping. Sometimes it takes mindfulness not to buy what we do not need. Before we go shopping, we make a shopping list of what we need to buy and determine that we shall only buy what is on it, because the marketeers and advertisements may be out to entice us to buy what we do not need and we will need to resist their bait. Many marketing and advertisement campaigns deceive us into thinking we need what we do not need. With mindfulness we can outwit them. Shopping mindfully, we can learn so much. We can look at whatever we want and investigate it without having to buy it. We can see where it was made and we can ask ourselves whether the producer received a fair reward or not for his labors.

Amidst the hustle and bustle around us, we can maintain our calmness. It is a holy season for Christians and for Jewish practitioners, a time to be connected to the spiritual light that is in each one of us as the light of day diminishes.

The celebration of the New Year in mindfulness can be very meaningful, too. All of us have a deep need for renewal, and the New Year celebration becomes the occasion for us to feel renewed. Saying goodbye to the year that has just passed means laying down our regrets as the foundation for our resolutions for the year that is just beginning. We can begin to prepare for the New Year one or two weeks in advance in ways that are described in Chapter 6. We can ask ourselves, "Is there anyone with whom I need to renew my relationship? Is there a telephone call I need to make? A letter I need to write?" That is renewal with the external world. Then there is the need to come back to ourselves and renew ourselves by our resolutions. We can write it down, offer it up to Jesus or God. It should be something simple, something doable. It could be a bit of a challenge, but knowing that it will bring joy to ourselves and the world, we want to take up that challenge, and we know we can do it.

11

Mindfulness
and
Gratitude

☙

When all thy mercies, O my God,
My rising soul surveys
Transported by the view I'm lost
In wonder, love and praise.

Ten thousand, thousand precious gifts,
My daily thanks employ.
Nor is the least a cheerful heart,
That tastes these gifts with joy.
　　　　　—JOSEPH ADDISON, 1672–1719

Can you imagine it: every day thousands and thousands of gifts? And yet it is true. Practicing mindfulness, we can receive thousands of precious gifts every day. We never need to feel self-pity. There is always something for which we can be grateful. You can sit with a pen and paper and write down all that you have to be grateful for. You may be surprised to discover ten thousand precious gifts. This is the practice of mindfulness of what we have to be grateful for. To begin with, there are our sense organs: our eyes, two precious jewels that bring us the shades and colors of the sunset or sunrise; our ears that bring us the song of the birds, the soughing of the wind in the trees, and the song of the brook; our noses that bring us the fragrance of the mountain, countryside, or sea air; our tongues that taste the fragrant herbs of Mother Earth.

In the United States people have a chance to practice gratitude once a year at Thanksgiving. In Europe there are harvest festivals in the autumn to thank God and the Earth for the harvest. All of us need to organize Thanksgiving ceremonies from time to time. We can be mindful of our gratitude to our parents, teachers, friends, and all beings in the animal, plant, and mineral worlds. Our parents have given us life and, in most circumstances, provided for us as we grew up. Even if our relationship with our parents has not been easy, we can always find something to feel grateful to our fathers and mothers for. If your parents are still alive, on their birthdays, you may like to write letters to them expressing your gratitude. At first you may think there are just one or two things, but as you put pen to paper, more and more things come to mind. Someone told me that on her father's seventieth birthday, she found seventy things to be grateful to him for. On a thanksgiving day all we need to keep reminding ourselves of is our gratitude. Maybe you will find that everyday can be a thanksgiving day.

There is a connection between feeling gratitude and praising God. In both cases, our hearts are filled with happiness and are lifted to a higher level. When we say that mindfulness is a source of happiness, we mean that by being mindful of what we have to be grateful for, we become happier people. Mindfulness is to be aware of all the precious things that are available to us. Our eyes are two jewels beyond price. Imagine you have lost your sight; if it were restored you would be the happiest person on Earth. The blue sky and the white clouds would be there again for you. Your feet that can still run or walk can bring you much joy, taking you on walks, touching the earth beneath them at every step. Your children grow up so fast, and to be able to express your gratitude to them brings us all much happiness. When your express gratitude to your children, you remember to let them know precisely which qualities and which of their actions you are grateful for. Then they know your gratitude is sincere.

Gratitude is a way of storing up wood for the winter. Those who live in the countryside find time in the summer and autumn to prepare wood for keeping warm in the winter when snow is on the ground. In the same way, we need to have moments of deep happiness that do not depend on consumption or outer circumstances but on our states of mind. These moments are stored in our memories, and when we come upon hard times, they are there to warm us and bring us relief.

12

Mindfulness
and
Driving the Car

◊

Some of us like to have a medallion of St. Christopher in our car. We feel that the saint is in our cars with us, and the saint drives very mindfully, bringing us safely to our destination. It reminds us that we are safe as long as we remain mindful as we drive. Once we are seated in the driver's seat, before we start our car, we can stop and breathe in and out three times. As we breathe like this, we are clear about our destination and our motivation for going there. Sometimes when our minds are troubled, we jump into our cars on an impulse, hoping to get away from it all. In fact, we do not have a destination we need to drive to. As we breathe in and out before we start the car, we may realize that the best thing we can do to calm our troubled minds is to take a mindful walk.

We remind ourselves to drive safely with love in our hearts. If anything untoward were to happen to us, we know it would be very painful for all our family and friends, so that even if we are driving on our own with no need to think of our passengers' safety, we do not want to take any unnecessary risks while driving. The most accidents are recorded where people are driving close to home on a familiar route. Because they have become so used to driving on that route, they are not fully aware, and if there has been some unexpected change, they do not respond quickly enough to it but keep driving as if everything was normal. Before we start our cars, we should remind ourselves that two-thirds of accidents occur close to home and that we want to drive carefully and with full awareness, even though we are not going far.

There is a mindfulness practice called mindfulness of the red light. Before I learned this practice, I would see the red light as a bit of an enemy and would wait impatiently for it to change. When you are mindful of the red light, you see it as a friend, encouraging you to sit back in the driver's or passenger seat and relax as you follow your breathing. "Breathing in, I smile. Breathing out, I release all tension." Now I am almost happier to see a red light than I am to see a green.

As a passenger you can enjoy the drive by following

your mindful breathing and dwelling in the present moment. You can support the driver with your mindfulness. For instance, when the driver is about to overtake, you can remain silent so the driver can give all her attention to this possibly dangerous maneuver.

13

Mindfulness and Mother Earth

∽

How lovely are your dwelling places,
  Yahweh Sabaoth.
My heart and my body cry out for joy to
  the living God.
Even the sparrow has found a home, the
  swallow a nest to rest.
Better one day in your courts than a
  thousand at my own devices.
              —PSALM 84

Often when I leave my desk and step outside the door, looking at the Earth and the sky, the first words that come to my mind are the words of Psalm 84. I do not think that the dwelling place of the living God is reserved for the future. If God is living, it is right here and now, and I greet it with a great sense of awe. The Earth is the dwelling place of God. The raindrop falling into the pond and the perfect concentric circles that it makes, if it is not the work of God, then what is it?

Many of us are actively wondering what we can best do to take care of the Earth. Maybe the first thing is to consume less, to be mindful of what we consume, especially the things we consume that do so much harm to the Earth. If we consume less, we shall have more time to be with nature and to be in nature.

The second thing is to change our ways of relating to Mother Earth. We practice to see her no longer as matter to be exploited but as a mother who needs to be protected. The Earth is not inert matter, but rather a living organism and spiritual being. We rejoice in her beauty and find time to be in nature and to plant trees. We strive to protect the Earth out of love and not out of fear. Of course, we are all very afraid of the degradation of the planet because it could mean that in fifty or sixty years there will be no more human life. But if we take action to save life on Earth out of fear, will that be beneficial action? If we think of times in the past when we acted out of fear, we will remember that our minds were not clear. We were in fight or flight mode.

But when we managed to calm our fears, we could see clearly what we needed to do or not to do. The first step is to calm our fears because the fears that lead us to fight are not nonviolent.

Parents and grandparents are particularly concerned for the future of their children. But it is the young people who worry most about global warming, and all the refuse left by human beings that is polluting the planet. They feel they are victims of their elders who have overconsumed in total lack of awareness of what they are doing to the ecosystem. How can we comfort our younger generation and help them be less afraid? The outlook is not good. We need to change our way of living quickly, and so many of us are still not awake to what is happening every day as far as Mother Earth and all the species that are part of her are concerned. On the other hand, there are so many things we can do, and just doing small things to contribute to caring for the Earth can already bring us happiness. Some people fly less, reduce energy consumption in their homes, build solar panels, buy as little plastic as possible. There is so much one individual can do.

As practitioners of mindfulness, we see the spiritual dimension as the very foundation. We help the young people to develop this dimension by living life deeply and meaningfully. Normally we think of time as an arrow that goes in a straight line in one dimension, but there is a depth-dimension to time. When we live the depth-dimension to time, we no longer measure time in terms of hours, days, and years. We go into the present moment deeply and touch a dimension beyond time. Our bodies can adopt the positions of sitting, lying, walking, standing, or kneeling. In any of these positions we can practice mindfulness of the positions of our body. We can choose whatever position is most comfortable for us and helps us to be focused.

Breathing in and out, I know I am standing (sitting) and I am standing (sitting) up straight between heaven and Earth. I know that I am a child of the Earth along with all the animal, plant, and mineral species that belong to our planet. I know that the human species has the capacity to be compassionate but can also be the most thoughtless and cruel of all species. As a human child of Mother Earth, I am determined to be the best that a human being can be. I know that if I am filled with fear about the future, I shall become paralyzed and not be able to do anything to help. I also know that if I act out of love, I shall nourish myself and others. So, I am going to help the Earth by developing my capacity to love, understand, and be fearless. This I do by calming my body and mind, bringing them into the present moment with the help of my mindful breath, not allowing my mind to wander into regions of fear and despair.

Every day I shall give myself the opportunity to be in touch with the wonders of this beautiful blue-green planet: the autumn leaves, the summer flowers, the winter frosts, and the spring renewal. I shall remember to hug a tree in order to receive its healing energy and to feel connected to the Earth. I shall do my part in practical ways. There are so many ways of behavior and consumption that can be positive for saving life on our planet. I shall join a group that is practicing nonviolent resistance to all that is being done to destroy the planet. I shall be a positive part of that group helping others to stay calm and awake and not carried away by anger. I know that my peaceful presence is the most important contribution I can make to the protest. I shall maintain the awareness that I and the Earth are one, and that those we are protesting against are, like us, children of the Earth. I shall look at myself and the Earth as two inseparable realities. I know that my health and the health of the Earth are interconnected in a wonderful way, and taking care of my body is at the same time taking care of the Earth. Especially when eating a meal, I shall see that the food that brings me health is the food that brings health to the Earth.

14

Mindfulness and Activism

∽

They will hammer their swords into ploughshares and their spears into sickles . . . no longer will they learn how to make war.

—ISAIAH 2:34

The path of mindfulness is one of nonviolence; so mindful activism is always nonviolent activism. We are not violent toward ourselves or toward others when we practice mindfulness. Sometimes we talk of mindfulness in terms of mere recognition. We recognize what is happening around us without judgment of whether that is good or bad, friend or enemy. For example, when we recognize we are not being mindful, we do not judge ourselves. We do not want to turn ourselves into a battlefield where the good fights against the evil. We recognize we are not being mindful and straightaway, without needing to make any effort, we will become mindful. We recognize that "we are feeling sad," and straightaway our sadness is embraced by our mindfulness so that it does not overwhelm us, even though it may stay for a while.

Another important aspect of mindfulness is mindfulness of suffering. We are led by our mindfulness of suffering to do something to alleviate the suffering. Here we could understand Holy Spirit as mindfulness of the suffering and the deep aspiration to do something to alleviate it. There is mindfulness of the suffering that makes the building of nuclear armaments possible and mindfulness of the suffering that these armaments could wreak on our planet Earth. We live in a world where there are enough nuclear armaments to destroy everything on the planet twenty times over, but most of us are not mindful of this. We could say that those who are mindful are led by the Holy Spirit.

None of us want to learn how to make war, but we know that wars do not just happen, and there is a process that leads to them. That process begins in our human species when we think, speak, or act in certain ways. We may not be at war now, but in our hearts, we may be preparing for war. As practitioners of mindfulness, we are aware of the suffering caused by war, and we do not want to think, speak, or act in such a way as would lead to war.

When I join a protest against war, killing, nuclear weapons, I visualize myself as a plough. In our own time people use very powerful ploughs with large steel blades that cut deep into the Earth. They little resemble the ploughs with which the prophet Isaiah or the Buddha were familiar. When I imagine myself as a plough, it is the kind of plough that is pulled by oxen and does not dig too deep into the Earth. It is a wooden plough. The Earth is light and golden brown, and my plough is preparing it so that seeds of goodness, beauty, and truth can be sown. The collective consciousness of the human species is an Earth where seeds can be sown.

In 1980, Fr. Daniel Berrigan and his brother, Philip Berrigan, a former Catholic priest, began the Plowshares movement with six others to demonstrate against nuclear weapons, inspired by the words of the prophets. Hammering nuclear missiles and submarines into ploughshares, using their own blood to pour on documents and weapons, they had to face many years of imprisonment.

There is a deep connection between spirituality and activism. In our Buddhist tradition, we often speak of mindfulness as holiness or the equivalent of the Holy Spirit. When put on trial for trespassing, entering security areas, doing damage to property, members of the Plowshares movement would talk of being led by the Holy Spirit.

> People who have been involved in plowshares actions have undertaken a process of intense spiritual preparation, nonviolence training and community formation, and have given careful consideration to the risks involved.[1]

> There is not going to be any real disarmament until there's a disarming of hearts. And so one puts oneself on the line to symbolically, but really, disarm the weapons in a hope and prayer that the action might be used by the Spirit of God to change minds and hearts. One puts oneself on the line—at risk and in jeopardy—to communicate the depth of commitment to that hope.[2]

Personally, for health reasons I would not risk arrest now. Though to the best of my ability, I would go to demonstrations. When I read or hear about how people

---

[1] Art Laffin, History of Plowshares Movement, October 22, 2019, https://www.nukeresister.org/2019/11/02/a-history-of-the-plowshares-movement-a-talk-by-art-laffin-october-22-2019/.

[2] Liz McAlister, *The Catholic Agitator*, November 1992.

put themselves on the line to communicate their deep commitment to disarmament, I am deeply moved and it has an immediate effect on my life. It deepens my own commitment to practice nonviolence in all my actions of body, speech, and mind. If an unkind thought toward my sister begins in my mind, I quickly transform it into kindness, simply because I am mindful of the fact that people are protesting, putting their well-being at risk to promote disarmament, and I cannot contribute to war by the slightest tremor of my unkind heart. For this reason, I know that those who protest and demonstrate nonviolently are having a good effect on the world and on the collective consciousness. Knowledge that there are human beings who, from a deeply spiritual motivation, undertake selfless action helps me not drown in despair when I see the situation of our world.

There is another deep connection of which we should be aware and that is the connection between inner and outer peace, between nuclear disarmament and disarming our hearts. In our family, our community, our workplace we can train ourselves every day to practice inner peace. That is why spiritual practice and activism cannot be two separate things.

First of all, you are active in bringing peace into your own heart. Secondly, you bring peace into your family and to those with whom you have daily contact. This peace can only ripple outward, and if you can do this, you can also be an activist in a movement like the Plowshares movement. In that movement, the other members are as dear to you as your blood brothers and sisters. You support each other in your practice of nonviolence so that you do not have to burn out or fall into despair.

15

Mindfulness
and
Death

☙

*All praise be yours, my Lord, for Sister
    Death,
From whose embrace no mortal can
    escape.
Laudato si, mi signore, per sora nostra
    morte corporale,
de la quale nullu homo vivente po skap-
    pare.*

—St. Francis of Assisi

*Are you able to contemplate your
death and the death of those closest
to you? Accepting the fact of death,*

> *we are freed to live more fully. In*
> *bereavement, give yourself time to*
> *grieve. When others mourn, let your*
> *love embrace them.*
> —FROM THE QUAKER *ADVICES*
> *AND QUERIES*

> *I assure you that unless a grain of*
> *wheat falls into the earth and dies,*
> *it can only be a single seed. But if it*
> *dies, it bears much fruit.*
> —JOHN 12:24

Mindfulness of dying is sometimes called remembrance of death. We remind ourselves that we are of the nature to die and that there is no escape from death. It is only natural that we have a deep-seated fear of death—often so deep that we do not recognize it. We are afraid of our own deaths and afraid of the death of our loved ones. From time to time, thoughts of our own mortality may come up, but our usual reaction is to push them away by turning our attention to something else: eating a piece of chocolate, turning on the television, picking up a magazine or a book. However, the fear does not lessen, and there will come a time when we are forced to recognize that we are going to die and our loved ones, too, are going to die. The benefit of contemplating our own death is that it forces us to live each moment of life we have left to us deeply. Knowing that our loved ones will die, we appreciate each precious moment we can be with them. If we believed that we would live forever, we would become bored with life and take it for granted.

But what is death? Do we know that thing of which we are so afraid? Can we look directly at our perception and concept of death and go beyond it? Indeed, death is an idea about nonexistence, about loss of everything. As Socrates said, we do not know what happens after the transition called death. We believe either that we shall continue in purgatory or heaven or that we shall become nothing. We have no real evidence of either these beliefs. All we can be sure of is that when we burn a piece of paper, it becomes ash, smoke, and heat, and we cannot make ash into anything.

Besides death, we are also very afraid of ill health, because ill health can lead to death. When the doctor gives a diagnosis of disease, she may also give us a prognosis of how long we have to live. The most difficult scenario is maybe to die suddenly in an accident without any preparation. It is indeed preferable to have a period of ill health before we die, because that is the time for us to be able to purify our hearts and to prepare for this transition. If the doctor gives us three months, we have three months to purify our heart. The prognosis is based on the average number of days and months that are left to people who have reached the same stage of the disease as we have, but everyone is different. Some people are given a prognosis of a few months and live for ten years or more. Of course, to die peacefully at an advanced age would be most people's preference, but how many of us enjoy that privilege? When we are growing old, we need to contemplate our own mortality, but it is best to prepare ourselves for our own and our loved ones' deaths while we are strong and in good health.

When you make the commitment in a marriage ceremony or otherwise to live with your partner until one of you dies, of course you do not want to think about the time of death. However it can be helpful to bear in mind that there will be a day when one of you dies. Psychologically, it can be devastating when someone you have lived with for many years as a partner dies. We can never be completely prepared, but we can take some steps that help us accept death. Those of us who recite the Hail Mary every day are reminded of our own impermanence when we say: *now and at the hour of our death.* We say those words knowing that we shall die and that those we love will die. Accepting that I and my loved one will die is one step, but the next step is to see that neither of us can become nothing. Before you were born, you were there and after you die you continue to be there. According to science cells are being born and dying at every moment. Psychologically you are constantly renewing yourself, as well as staying the same. So you are a process of birth and death, even while you are alive. You are not exactly the same person as you were yesterday and the same is true of your loved one.

So it is helpful to ask your loved one from time to time: "Before you were born were you there? In what form were you there? After you die, will you be there? In what form will you be there?" By asking these questions we accept that we shall not always be together in the physical form we are used to, but we shall not become nothing.

Death is going back to the source. Our bodies will go back to the planet Earth, which is always there to embrace us; our soul[1] will go back to our loved ones. We may rest in God or in our spiritual ancestors and go forward in our descendants. We are as a cloud that comes from water and goes back to water. We cannot remain forever as a cloud. If in my daily life, I have been able to face the fear of death when it arises; then at the point of death, I can also face that fear with calm and know that it is just fear. I can entrust myself to Mother Mary, to Jesus Christ, my community of practice, my root teacher.

From time to time, we accompany a friend or a loved one who is dying. Our calm, nonfearing presence is the best gift we can bring to the one who is dying. The

---

[1]Our soul could also be our spirit made of *feelings, emotions, perceptions, thoughts,* and *consciousness.*

mindful breathing with words of prayer said quietly to ourselves can make the energy in the room peaceful. Gentle massage of the feet and hands is helpful. What we say can be an obstacle or a benefit to the dying person, so we need to be very mindful of what we say and watch carefully the reaction of the dying person to our words. We can recount some beautiful events from the dying person's life. For example, "Do you remember the times when you took the whole family on holiday and we had so much fun together?"

Reconciliation is very important at this time. If we hear that a relative with whom we have not yet made peace is dying, we have a chance to practice forgiveness before it is too late. Seeing a family member or friend on her deathbed is often enough to arouse compassion in our hearts and to bring loving words of apology or forgiveness to our lips. We can contemplate the beautiful qualities that we appreciate in that person before we go to visit her. Absence of any regret makes for much less grief.

Sometimes a doctor who has not been able to cure a patient will feel ashamed and out of all humility will say, "I am sorry. I cannot do any more for her." There is always something a doctor can do. The peaceful presence full of compassion of a doctor or nurse who sits with the one who is dying is doing a great deal.

Even after the heart has stopped beating and there is

no longer any breath, we can continue to speak to the person who has died, and maybe he can hear. The person may even be able to see.

It is best not to be too quick to move the body after death. Leave at least a few hours for the person to be undisturbed. This period is followed by a time of transition for the one who has died and for those of us who remain. The transition can last forty-nine days, a hundred days, or a year. The peace and the joy of those of us who are living are also the peace and joy of the one who has died. Mindful grieving means that we allow ourselves to grieve, but at the same time, our mindful steps and breath keep us peaceful. We can make a small altar with a photograph of the deceased one. We can come there to light a candle or read a sacred text, feeling the presence of our loved one as we read.

It is said that if our grieving is destructive to our bodies and minds, it is an obstacle to the peace of the one we have lost. Many different, unexpected feelings can come up when we lose someone we love. The most common is regret: thoughts like if I had done this, he could have lived longer; if she were here, I could share this with her. Some of us feel anger with the person for dying and leaving us. When regret or anger arise, we can recognize them by greeting them: *hello, regret (anger). I know you are there.* There is also the inability to accept that our loved one has died. Whatever thought or emotion comes up wants to be embraced and not repressed, recognized and not pushed away. We need time and space to do this. We also need friends to support us. Sometimes episodic depression can set in. If this happens, we need to practice mindfulness of depression. In fact, to have depressed feelings come up from time to time after someone very close to us dies is a natural part of the grieving process. When we allow ourselves to experience and observe these depressed feelings, then they will go away when they have served their purpose in our loss.

If episodic depression, "which may be characterized by a long-term and excessively depressed state,"[2] turns into clinical depression you should seek professional help and take medication, but medication is not enough on its own. Depression comes in waves, and with mindfulness you recognize those waves as they begin. You observe where you feel the depression in your body. You observe the thoughts you were having when the waves of depression began. With this practice, you begin to understand your depression, and with understanding you can transform it. You send the energy of your mindful breathing to the part of your body that is holding the depression.

---

[2]Elisabeth Kübler-Ross and David Kessler, *On Grief and Grieving: Finding the Meaning of Grief through the Five Stages of Loss* (New York: Scribner, 2014).

There are other activities that help: the kind of exercise you really enjoy, walking in nature, painting, making jam, and even taking a bath. Negative thinking always fuels depression. If you can put your whole attention on mindful breathing, you do not need to think, and you will feel much better. Do not be too convinced that your loved ones are no longer there. Always be mindful of the fact that they have not gone anywhere and are available to you, although you cannot see them.

Recently I heard that at least fourteen priests in the Maryknoll community[3] had succumbed to the coronavirus. Many feelings came up in me, just as when I heard the news of the lives lost in the tsunamis of 2004 and 2011. One of those feelings was an instinctual observation from my self-survival complex: well, anyway it was not me, it was not the sisters in my community that died. On recognizing that thought, I have to breathe and stop and look again. "No, I die with them and they also continue to live in me." With that reflection I feel much better. I am in touch with something that is nearer to the truth and I am not trying to run away from death. I feel compassion for us all as a human species.

---

[3]Maryknoll Fathers and Brothers is a US Catholic order of priests and brothers that devotes itself to spreading the LOVE of God among those in need across Asia, Africa, and Latin America.

Mindfulness of Ancestors and Descendants

Mindfulness of ancestors and descendants is a cure for many imbalances of body and mind; it is also a source of immense energy.

We are not born from nothing and we do not die into nothing. We are the continuation of our mother, father, grandparents, and all our ancestors. Our children, grand-children, great-grandchildren, and future generations continue us. In many cultures, awareness of forebears is a very important aspect of spiritual life. Thanks to my contact, through Thay, with the Vietnamese culture, I have come to value this practice.

When Christian missionaries first came to Vietnam, they bid their converts destroy their ancestral altars. This was based on a misunderstanding. They thought that the Vietnamese were worshipping their ancestors, but an ancestral altar is not for worship in the way we worship God or in the usual sense of the word. There is nothing in Christianity that is contrary to the mindful awareness of ancestors. Jesus Christ must have been very aware of his ancestral lineage as we see from the first chapter of Matthew and the third chapter of Luke.

Every year I remember the days that my father and my mother died and ask my community to help me perform a memorial ceremony. I see clearly that my father and mother are in me, and I am their continuation as we chant the scriptures.

An ancestral altar can be very simple: a photograph of your deceased parents, grandparents, or great-grand-parents, a candle, and some flowers. It can be placed in the entrance hall to your home, your study, or your meditation room. You come there not to worship your ancestors, but rather to be in touch with them and to recognize that they are your roots. Just as a tree needs roots, we, humans, need awareness of our ancestors as our roots. Healing energy comes from this awareness. Once you have come before your ancestors, you can share with them what is happening in your family (your family members are also their descendants), at work, and so on. You can tell them of the challenges you may be facing and ask for their support.

If it is not appropriate for you to make an ancestral altar in your home, there is a deeper practice, which is to be mindful of your body as an altar for your ancestors. Concretely your body is your ancestors. It is their genetic continuation. You take care of your body as you would take care of an altar, in order to remember your ancestors who have made your life possible. This means you exercise and you consume in such a way that keeps your body a sacred place.

Our blood ancestors are not the only source of our lives. We also have spiritual ancestors who transmit to us the spiritual direction that our life takes. Jesus was also aware of his spiritual ancestors from an early age: "Did you not know that I must be in my father's house?" (Luke 2:49). Our blood ancestors are one of our roots, and our spiritual ancestors are no less important a root. No doubt as a Christian, Jesus is your most important spiritual ancestor. The teachings of Jesus have come down to us by means of an unbroken lineage from Jesus Christ to the Apostles, to Paul, to the Desert Fathers, and so on right up to our own spiritual teachers of the present. We can see ourselves as being at the midpoint of a line of ancestors and descendants, responsible for handing down to our spiritual descendants that which we receive from our spiritual ancestors. Seeing our spiritual ancestors in ourselves, we see clearly our direction in life as their continuation.

Mindful of our blood and our spiritual ancestors, we shall see their qualities that we want to continue, and we shall also see their shortcomings. We cannot reject our ancestors, because of their mistaken ways. Who are we, who are by no means perfect, to do that? Our ancestors, our father and mother, are in us because they have transmitted many qualities to us not only through the genes but also in their ways of thinking. They have transmitted their joy of life to us and also their pain and wounds of war and other events. We accept all our ancestors as they are, and we feel well because, by accepting them, we are accepting ourselves. When we transform and heal a wound in ourselves, we heal this wound for our ancestors at the same time. They hope for us to continue the path of love and healing for them. If I am able to transform some of the wounds in me into understanding and compassion, both my ancestors and descendants will benefit.

In a retreat I attended in 1986, we were invited to an ancestral memorial ceremony. We were told to bear in mind two ancestors in the ceremony and write down their names, which were placed on a board. I chose my maternal grandmother with whom I had not had such a good relationship. I resented her somewhat for what I considered to be her unethical life. In the retreat, we were told that our perception of our ancestors is like our perception of the moon; sometimes we see it as waxing and sometimes waning. In fact, it is always the moon.

Sometimes we see our ancestors as good and sometimes as bad, but in fact, they are always our ancestors. For the first time, I could accept my grandmother as she was and see myself as her continuation. This gave me greater acceptance of myself.

The same is true of my blood descendants, my nephews, nieces, grandnephews and -nieces, and my spiritual descendants, students, and fellow practitioners. Some of them, in my eyes, are doing well, and others meet with my disapproval. Mindful of the fact that I am not perfect, I can accept them all as they are.

17

Mindfulness
and
Total Relaxation

∽

*Martha, you worry and fret about
so many things, and yet few are
needed. Indeed only one.*
—LUKE 10:41

Our Lord encourages Martha to let go of all her concerns as far as serving Him are concerned. The time when
Jesus was in her house was a precious time to be in touch
with the true teachings. There are times when we need
to let go of all our activities and just do one thing. Total
relaxation is a way of letting go of all the occupations of
body, speech, and mind; and the one thing we do is relax.

When I lived in India, I would watch the local people

who came past the monastery on their way to a market. They would come on foot with a mule carrying their wares. They stopped and asked for water to drink. They made themselves comfortable sitting on the ground and would stay for an hour or two doing absolutely nothing. In our civilization we have lost this capacity to do nothing.

Our present civilization can only be called civilized if we know how to relax. We can learn how to make our  body as relaxed as a cat lying in the sunshine, which is soft due to the lack of tension in its muscles. During the day at work, we can build up so much tension in our bodies and minds, and there has to be a way for us to let go of it. Otherwise the tension will accumulate and make us unwell.

Today when you come home from work, instead of beginning your evening activities straightaway, give yourself eleven or twelve minutes minimum of total relaxation. As soon as you have taken off your coat, you can go to a spot in your home that is calm and clean and lie down on the floor on a blanket. If it is cold, you can cover yourself with another blanket because when cold, it is difficult to relax. Lie flat on your back, your arms a little apart from the body with the palms turned upward, the heels close together but the feet allowed to fall outward away from each other. Close your eyes; you can cover them with a piece of dark cloth if you wish. Relax your lower jaw so that it hangs loose. Keep the tongue and the pupils of the eyes still without disturbance. Follow your breathing deeply so that you can feel your abdomen rising and falling as you breathe in and out. First be aware of each of the parts of the body that are in contact with the floor. Next you can scan your body from your toes to your head and relax the different parts. Feel as if your body is sinking into the floor beneath you. Allow the tensions and resistance to fall away into the floor and all the events of the day that is past to drop away from you. Let go, let go of everything so that only your deep and mindful breathing stays as your anchor.

If you are a beginner and find it difficult to let go, you can use a relaxing piece of music to help you, but gradually you can learn to relax without the help of music.

The lying down position may be the most relaxing position, but we can also learn to relax as we are sitting, standing, or walking. It is beneficial to do so because the times when we most need to relax may come when it is not possible to lie down. When sitting at our desks, we can, from time to time, close our eyes and breathe deeply, stopping all our thinking for at least three in-breaths and out-breaths, feel the tension in our body, and let it go.

When, at any time, we feel we have been in a stressful situation, we can help the parasympathetic nervous system, the part of the system that relaxes us, to operate, by means of a very simple exercise. It is not beneficial to allow the stress to last any longer than it needs to, because accumulated stress leads to illness. Sitting on our chairs or lying on our beds, we clench our fists on the in-breath, and on the out-breath we open up our hands completely, letting go of all the tension. On the in-breath, we feel the tension, and on the out-breath, we slowly unclench our fists, letting go of more and more tension all the time, until we completely outstretch our fingers.

You can use the following instructions to guide your practice of relaxation in the supine position. The part in italics can be practiced when you only have ten minutes. The other part can be practiced as well when you have thirty minutes or longer.

∾

Allow your body to lie very peacefully. You have nothing to do other than to enjoy relaxing.

Remember the times in the past when you have felt completely relaxed and have confidence that you can relax now.

As you breathe in and out, feel your abdomen rising and falling. At first give all your attention to your abdomen.

Then feel the parts of your body that are in touch with the ground underneath you.

Feel your heels, the back of your calves, knees, and thighs. Feel your bottom, lower back, middle back, upper back, shoulders, and arms. Feel the back of your head where it touches the ground. With each breath feel how you sink deeper and deeper into the ground and how tensions and worries fall away.

Let go of all your thinking, and let yourself sink deeper into the ground.

Breathing in and out, feel your feet, first your left foot and then your right foot.

As you breathe in and out, allow your feet to relax, first the left and then the right foot.

Breathing in, send love to your feet. Breathing out, smile to your feet.

Breathing in and out, feel your legs, first the left leg, then the right leg.

Feel the whole length of your legs, beginning with the ankle until the hip.

Allow both legs to be totally relaxed.

When you feel some tension somewhere in your legs, take time to release it and let both legs sink deep into the ground.

Breathing in, send your love to both legs. Breathing out, smile to both legs.

Breathing in and out, feel your lower abdomen. Release tension in your lower abdomen. Send your love and smile to your lower abdomen.

Breathing in and out, feel your liver. Send your love and smile to your liver. Feel your liver functioning without stress, with the support of your mindfulness.

Breathing in and out, feel your kidneys. Send your love and smile to your kidneys. Feel your kidneys functioning without stress, with the support of your mindfulness.

Breathing in and out, feel your heart. Feel how wonderful it is that your heart is beating regularly in your breast. Feel your heart functioning without stress with the support of your mindfulness.

With each in-breath, feel love for your heart. With each out-breath, smile to your heart in thankfulness.

Breathing in and out, bring your attention to your back. Feel the lower back, then the middle back, and then the upper back. Notice any tension that you might be holding in your back. Let the tension sink out of your back into the floor.

Breathing in, send your love to your back. Breathing out, smile to your back in gratitude.

Breathing in and out, be aware of your shoulders. Allow the tension in your shoulders to sink away into the floor beneath you. Send your tender loving-care to your shoulders.

Breathing in and out, feel your arms from the shoulder to the wrist, first your right arm and then your left arm. Be aware of the upper arm, the elbow, and the forearm. With each out-breath, allow your arms to relax, letting the tensions fall away. Let your arms rest wholly on the ground.

Breathing in and out, feel your hands, first the left hand and then the right hand. Let go of any tensions in your hands. Feel every finger, the thumb, index finger, middle finger, ring finger, and little finger. Let each finger of each hand relax one by one. Feel how lucky you are to have two hands and allow every cell in each hand to relax.

Breathing in and out, be aware of your face. Allow each of the small muscles in your face to be totally re-laxed by smiling gently. Release all the tensions from the muscles around your mouth, eyes, and forehead. Allow your eyes to rest and sink deep into their sockets.

Breathing in and out, feel your whole body. Enjoy the feeling of relaxation that is in your body as you lie peacefully on the floor. Feel compassion for your body, smile to your body, and vow to take good care of it.

Feel the self-healing capacities in your body as you are mindful and relaxed. Be grateful for every cell in your body. Let your body relax completely and let go; let go of everything.

Slowly move your toes and fingers, then your arms and legs. Stretch. Bring your arms up over your head and stretch them. Now bring your knees up toward your chest. Turn your head to the right and bring your knees down to the left. Then turn your head to the left and bring your knees down to the right. Roll from side to side several times and open your eyes slowly. Give yourself plenty of time to sit up slowly.[1]

[1]There are a number of total relaxation audio recordings on the Plum Village App available for free download, which you can use to practice.

18

Mindfulness in Times of Ill Health

☙

*Neither he nor his parents sinned.
. . . He was born blind so that the
words of God might be revealed in
him.*

—JOHN 9:3

The wonderful thing about ill health is that it gives us a chance to learn about our bodies. Before falling ill, we did not take the time to understand our bodies, and we may have done things that have led to our present ill health. It is clear from the teachings of the gospels, the many miracles of healing that Jesus performed, that we should not think of ill health as a punishment from

God. We should not say, "Why do I have to bear this sickness? I have lived a healthy, wholesome life!" Rather than blaming God for letting this happen, we take it as an opportunity for the glory of God to be realized, which means an opportunity to heal our whole being: bodies, minds, and spirits.

Our bodies are truly wonderful instruments. We hesitate to use the word *instrument* because instruments are manmade, and our bodies are something that has evolved over millions of years: very subtle, constantly changing and adapting to their environment. When we fall sick, we do not need to lose faith in our bodies. In fact, we can find a deeper faith in it than the faith we had before. That faith comes when we experience our bodies healing themselves. We have all observed how when we cut our finger, it will heal itself in a wonderful way. We just need to keep it clean and still. Sometimes it is best to do nothing, in other words, just to rest. A sick animal will lie down in a quiet place and let its body take care of itself. At the very least, on falling ill, we do not immediately engage in all kinds of activity. We take the opportunity to rest as much as possible, both physically and mentally, giving our bodies and minds a chance to heal.

We learn the subtle intricacies of our bodies and how all parts are interrelated. A body is the most wonderful example of interrelationship. It is not separate from the mind and the spirit. Our ill health could have begun with stress, fear, anxiety, and sorrow. We did not know how to handle these emotions, and they cause blockages in the energies that flow through our bodies. We may have eaten the wrong food, failed to exercise our bodies regularly, or exercised them in the wrong way. The pollution of the environment by human beings is also a major cause of ill health. Now we  have a chance to listen to our bodies and let them tell us what they really need. We can talk to our hearts and the other organs of our bodies. As we lay our hands on the part of our bodies where the organs lie, we ask the organs what we can do to help them, and if we are still enough, the answer will come from an intuitive wisdom deep within. Sending our love and our mindful breathing to a part of our body that is in trouble, after ten or twenty minutes, nearly always brings some relief.

It is true that the technology of modern Western medicine has saved many lives, but we can learn not to overrely on doctors and nurses. We can see that the doctor and the patient collaborate together. The truth is that the body knows how to heal itself, and the doctor is there to empower the self-healing in the patient. We could say that the doctor does 50 percent and the patient has to do the other 50 percent. The good news is that every moment is a moment of change in our bodies, and so can be a moment of healing. Cells are constantly being born and dying. Mindfulness of the body and of the feelings is the key, because it is an awareness of what is happening in us from moment to moment. With some help and advice from a good doctor, we can begin to heal ourselves.

You can be aware of what is going right in your body, not just what is going wrong. Just as in your garden there may be one or two trees that are sick, but many other trees are healthy. You can still enjoy the healthy trees. In times of sickness, you can call to mind your ancestors and relatives who have lived to a ripe old age and remember that those long-life genes are also in you.

In recent times we hear about integrative medicine that heals bodies, minds, and souls together. Mindfulness becomes the key in this kind of healing. We are mindful of our bodies, our feelings, perceptions, and emotions. Mindfulness of our bodies means we become aware where our energy is blocked. We can do this on our own and call on the help of the health-care professional if needed. Then we become aware of our feelings. They can be pleasant or painful. While we dwell in mindfulness, we are not carried away by the pleasure or the pain. If we recognize the pleasant feelings are healing us, we keep it in our awareness as long as possible. If the pleasant feelings are causing us excitement or anxiety, we use our breathing to calm them. We are mindful of our perceptions, our view of the world: whether it is optimistic or pessimistic and whether it leads to loving-kindness or aversion. When we recognize thoughts or perceptions that heal us, we keep them in our awareness as long as possible. When we recognize thoughts or perceptions that cause us pain or increase our anxiety, we are careful not to keep thinking those thoughts. We are mindful of our emotional states and how they are influencing our health. We recognize restlessness, anxiety, and stress, and how they are directly responsible for unease and discomfort in our bodies. We do our best to stop and to breathe and walk mindfully in order for the parasympathetic nervous system to operate. This kind of mindfulness is both preventative and curative medicine.

19

Mindfulness of Love

❧

Love your enemies, do good to those
who hate you, pray for those who
treat you badly. If you love those who
love you, what credit can you expect?
—LUKE 6:27, 32

The word *love* sometimes loses its deep meaning. We talk about lovesick, falling in love, loving chocolate, loving the seaside. So sometimes we want to write the word *love*, which does not have any of the above meanings, in a different way. Easiest may be to use the word *mindfully* and only use it when you are talking about the love that is born of understanding. If you want to know whether your love is true love, you can examine it in the following way. Do I want and am I able to do what makes the other person happy? Do I want the other person not to suffer, and am I able to do things that help that person suffer less? Does my love bring me and the other joy? Is my love inclusive? Is my heart large enough to include those I find difficult to love?

The practice of love in mindfulness is to love those whom we consider unlovable, and to change an enemy into a friend, as well as to love better those we already love. Love can change into hate and hate can change into love. We practice mindfulness so that love can last and hate can come to an end. The basis of all love is understanding and the ability to change our perception about ourselves and about the other person. If we say we want to love someone but we do not understand them, our wish will not be realized. Love is not an intention but an understanding of ourselves and the other in the present moment. We all need to love and to understand, as we all need to be loved and understood. When we pray for those who treat us badly, we can pray that they be happy, safe, and free from accident, because that is what we all want for ourselves. Before we can pray like that, we need to realize how much we ourselves want happiness and safety. So, we may begin our prayer by praying for ourselves, wishing that I myself may be happy, safe, and free from accident. If we do not want happiness for ourselves, we cannot want it for others.

How we think about others is very important. Sometimes we consider that thinking is what happens in our head and no one else will know about it, but looking deeply, we shall see that thinking is at the root of our verbal and bodily actions. The way we think does not stay in our heads but goes out into every cell of our bodies and into the world. Others can sense and feel our energy of anger, irritation, or love, even if we do not say or do anything. A compassionate thought can heal ourselves and heal the world. A thought of hatred can make us sick and harm the world.

You can train yourself to think lovingly about yourself and about others. In the following exercise the *power* and healing of the thoughts come when you are in a state of calm and peace, with concentration. You sit quietly, aware of your breathing, and then repeat the phrases below with your in-breath and out-breath, opening your heart and feeling this wish deep within, resonating in you. It is not just *thinking* in the common sense of the word; it is closer to prayer. Always begin by wishing these thoughts for yourself. If you only do that much, it is already very healing. When you feel filled with love for yourself, you can continue to wish for another. The prayer is not a repetition of empty words. You feel that these are words that you need and want for yourself deeply. Only then can you see that the words are what the other person needs and wants. You do not need to practice the whole exercise at the same time, but rather choose what is most

appropriate. You may also want to include other wishes
for yourself and others.

> May I (you) be happy, peaceful, and
> light in body and spirit.
> May I (you) be safe and free from ac-
> cident.
> May I (you) be free from anxiety, fear,
> and anger.

> May I (you) learn to look at myself
> (yourself) with the eyes of under-
> standing.
> May I (you) identify the seeds of suf-
> fering in myself (yourself).
> May I (you) identify and develop the
> seeds of joy in myself (yourself).

> May I (you) nourish the joy in me (you)
> every day.
> May I (you) live fresh, solid, and free.
> May I (you) not be attached or averse
> and also not indifferent.[1]

Part II

Double-Belonging

The second part of this book looks further into the question of double-belonging and the question of what different spiritual paths can have in common. It is a miscellany of various insights and observations over my years of practicing Buddhism and Christianity.

If people ask me which religious tradition I belong to, it is a very difficult question to answer. Whatever I say does not sound quite right. Once a Chinese Zen master (Mazu Daoyi) said, "Whenever I am forced to say the word 'Buddha,' I need to go down to the river and rinse my mouth for three days." An intelligent disciple rebutted, "Venerable sir, whenever I hear you say the word Buddha, I need to put my hands over my ears and run away." Why were the Zen master and his disciple loathe to use the word *Buddha*? It was because whoever heard the word *Buddha* would immediately give rise to misconceptions about what is meant by Buddha. When I say that

I am a Buddhist nun, I have the feeling that the person listening has a misconception of what I mean. I do not want to be put in the box that is labeled Buddhism or Christianity or any other –ism. Thay has said, "I am a Buddhist, but I am not caught in Buddhism."

Historically, and in our own time, religious faith has too often been a divisive factor in the garden of humanity. More than anything, I want our spiritual practice, whatever it may be, to unite us to other spiritual practitioners, whatever their paths may be. I do not feel close to someone because they hold to the same religious path as I do. I was moved when I read the essay "Nhat Hanh Is My Brother" by Thomas Merton:[1] "Thich Nhat Hanh is more my brother than many who are nearer to me in race and nationality . . . We are both monks, and we have lived the monastic life about the same number of years . . . It is vitally important that such bonds (of friendship) be admitted. They are bonds of a new solidarity, and a new brotherhood, which is beginning to be evident on all five continents, and which cuts across all political, religious, and culture lines." In our own time, it is important to realize that we belong to a great human family where every spiritual path can offer its best and, at the

---

[1] Thomas Merton, "Nhat Hanh Is My Brother," in *Faith and Violence* (Notre Dame, IN: University of Notre Dame Press, 1968), 106–108.

same time, be open to others' viewpoints. I am first of all a human being, a flower in the garden of humanity. I belong to the human race, and at the same time I see that the human race is only there because all the other species, animal, vegetable, and mineral, are there. I am humble about being a human. I know our species has defects, but it also has wonderful potentials that are manifested in the lives of great beings of which Jesus Christ and Sakyamuni Buddha are only just two examples.

We can look in order to find the qualities that are most important in the human race for us to be able to continue as a beautiful species. All of us humans have the capacity to feel awe, gratitude, and compassion. These emotions are something that can unite us, although our feelings of awe and gratitude are sometimes so deep that it is not possible to express them in words. We feel awe and gratitude in the face of nature, the universe, and of God. Thay has written,[2]

> Every advance in our understanding of ourselves, nature, and our place in the cosmos deepens our reverence and love. To understand and to love are two fundamental needs . . . Humanity needs a kind

---

[2]Thich Nhat Hanh, *Love Letter to the Earth* (New York: Parallax Press, 2013), 139.

of spirituality that we can all practise together. Dogmatism and fanaticism have been the cause of great separation and war.

If existing religions and philosophies, as well as science, can make an effort to go in this direction, it would be possible to establish a cosmic religion, based not on myth, belief, or dogma, but on evidence and the insight of interbeing, and that would be a giant leap forward for humankind.

20

Interbeing

☙

Here is a word that is not yet in the dictionary but that I have become familiar with over many years as a student of Thay: *interbeing*. It simply means that I cannot be on my own; I have to be with others. It also means that everything in the world must rely on others. The rose cannot be without the rain, the sunshine, the earth, and the gardener. The good cannot be without the evil. The suffering cannot be without the happiness.

There are clear examples in the gospels that Jesus taught and had a deep understanding of interbeing. For example, in John 14:10, "Anyone who has seen me has seen the Father," and then, "I am in the Father and the Father is in me." This is a particular kind of interbeing. It is interbeing, if you like, on a vertical plane. It is interbeing between the phenomenological and ontological realities. The Father belongs to the ontological, Jesus to the phenomenological. We say that Jesus belongs to the phenomenological because Jesus appears to the world in flesh and blood. We read at verse 20, "You will know that I am in my Father and you in me and I am in you."

"I am in you," is another kind of interbeing. It is the interbeing on the horizontal plane between the phenomenological and the phenomenological. At Matthew 26: 26–28, to say of the bread, "This is my body," and of the wine, "This is my blood," is also a deep understanding of interbeing between the phenomenological and the phenomenological. The teaching at John 14:20 includes both kinds of interbeing. If Jesus is in the Father and the disciples are in Jesus then the disciples must also be in the Father. So, the disciples also enjoy interbeing on the vertical plane. As disciples of Jesus who practice according to the teachings of forgiveness, understanding, and love, we also enjoy interbeing with the Father.

The important thing to recognize is the presence of Jesus and of the Father in your consciousness at every possible moment. This kind of interbeing is both vertical and horizontal. It is wonderful to observe the interbeing between creator and creation. It is said that when St. Francis of Assisi was able to do this, his joy was so great that he ran through the streets of Assisi singing.

In our daily lives we may not yet be used to looking at life in terms of interbeing, so we can train ourselves. A child who is angry with his father can say things like,

"That man! I do not consider him to be my father." A parent who is angry at her child can say, "If you do things like that, I no longer consider you to be my daughter." Father, mother, daughter, and son all *inter-are*. We cannot take them out of each other. In order to be happy, we need our father or our son to be happy. A father is only a father because he has a son. A daughter is only a daughter because she has a mother. The father cannot be truly happy if the son is not happy. The daughter cannot be happy if the mother is not happy.

As students in the school or the university, we may be taught to compete with each other. In the workplace, we may continue this habit of competing. In our lives as adults, we can continue to compare ourselves with others, which can bring us much suffering. If we have the insight of interbeing, the success of others becomes our own success. We learn to see that whether we succeed or fail, it is not a matter for our separate self. If we do well, it is because we *inter-are* with elements that make doing well possible. If we fail it is because we *inter-are* with elements that help us to fail. Our personal success or failure is no longer important. If someone praises us, we can accept the praise. We do not need false modesty. Nevertheless, we say to ourselves, "That is my father's or mother's genes or my teacher's teaching that has made this possible in me." When we fail, we see that this is our genetic heritage or our education that has made this failure possible in us.

The deepest truth cannot be expressed. It lies beyond concepts and words, but it can be approached by concepts and words. The insight into interbeing is the approach we can take in order to realize the truth that lies beyond words. We now know that in our bodies are the dust of the stars and the mitochondria that were there millions of years before the human body manifested. Our bodies are the coming together of so many elements in a wonderful way that we cannot put into words or understand intellectually. So, we can call it the creation of God.

21

God

Some people ask whether there is an equivalent to God in Buddhism. Normally we think of Christianity as a theistic and Buddhism as an atheistic spiritual path. The human being has a deep need for the devotional, an object to worship. A Buddhist also has this need, and so it happens sometimes that the Buddha is elevated to the status of a god, who can be worshipped, which is very far from what the Buddha taught. The feeling of devotion can help us lead an ethical life, and can bring us peace and comfort in times of difficulty. However, the feeling of devotion is not all there is to the spiritual path. There is the aspect of going deeply into and understanding the nature of reality as an important part of the spiritual path. We want to understand what is the nature of God and the nature of creation.

In the following quote from the Buddha, I have substituted the word *God* for the word *Emptiness*:

The nature of God is not different from the nature of all phenomena because all phenomena come from God. God does not belong to the plain of being and non-being, does not lie in the framework of wrong perceptions, is not marked by birth or death and transcends all views. Why? God cannot be found in space, does not have a form and cannot be conceived of. God has not been born and cannot be grasped by the intellect. Because God cannot be grasped, God embraces all phenomena and dwells only in non-discursive, nondiscriminative wisdom.[1]

Reading this, you may feel you are reading the words of a Christian mystic. For the mystic, God cannot be caught in ideas of being and nonbeing. Whatever is being has the possibility of becoming nonbeing, so God must transcend being and nonbeing. To be mindful of God is to touch the nature of reality. God does not lie outside of creation. If you can touch the flower deeply in its wondrous beauty, you can touch God. In a retreat at Nottingham University, Thay said, "If we can put God back in the right place, we can save the world from the spiritual crisis it faces at the present time." The crisis is

---

[1]Taisho 104.

that you are not able to see God in yourself or in your enemy. This can lead to the belief that God wants the destruction of your enemy or that God is on our side. It is a tremendous relief not to need the written or the spoken word to prove God exists or does not exist, because God belongs to that aspect of reality that transcends concepts of being or nonbeing, inside or outside. Rather than debate about whether God exists or not, you can use your energy to be in touch with God in all that is around you.

The German theologian Paul Tillich said that God is not a person, but not less than a person. This means that whatever we say in ontological or epistemological terms about God, it is not enough to satisfy the human needs for a personal relationship with God. Jesus, the Son of Man, is the human being who embodies the finest qualities that humankind can manifest so that we can relate to God in a personal way. We cannot imagine God without Jesus or the patriarchs and matriarchs.

As human beings we need human exemplars. When Thay invested me as abbess of the Green Mountain Dharma Center in Vermont, USA,[2] he gave me a calligraphy that read, "Representing the Buddha." I was a little embarrassed, because I felt my unworthiness. Could I truly represent the Buddha? When I was a child, I wanted to

---

[2] It has now moved to Blue Cliff Monastery, New York State.

represent Jesus. A priest disillusioned me of this aspiration. Feeling unworthy can have a positive aspect, if it keeps us humble; but it is an obstacle, if it stops us doing what we most want to do. Jesus and the Buddha so much need ambassadors or representatives on Earth. My teacher has represented the Buddha for me, so I need to do the best to represent the Buddha for my descendants in religion.

I have needed a teacher very much in my spiritual life; someone who is a human being and can manifest compassion and deep understanding. This gives me confidence that I can do that too. In the beginning, I thought that one day I would be able to replace Thay; I would be able to do for others what Thay had done for me. It took me several years to realize that I am a unique human being, and I have to use what I have received from my ancestors in order to realize awakening. I cannot become a clone of Thay however hard I try. Nor can I become a clone of the Buddha or Jesus Christ, but I can represent them. Thay has said that a good teacher is not someone who makes you dependent on him, but rather someone who can show you the teacher in yourself so that you do not need to be dependent. A parent bird needs to teach its young to fly but only at the right time when the wings are strong enough. Once the parent bird has transmitted its experience to the child bird it can fly on its own in the vast sky.

We are called on to seek out those who represent Christ or the Buddha in the beginning, but then we are called on to represent Christ or the Buddha ourselves.

Today a mother, her daughters, and helpers visited our monastery. The mother had heard about Thay and mindfulness. She had been diagnosed with ALS,[3] a form of motor neurone disease, and she was told she did not have much longer to live. She could not walk, and it was very difficult for her to speak. She had a tablet on which she could write. Someone suggested that we chant the name of Avalokiteśvara bodhisattva[4] to help her feel more peaceful. While we were chanting it crossed my mind that I was Avalokiteśvara, the woman with ALS was Avalokiteśvara, and Avalokiteśvara was near us in an invisible form, too. Later on, I wondered how I would have felt if I believed in a creator God outside of creation. I would have found it difficult to accept that an all-loving creator could have created diseases like this. I could not accept a creator God who is outside of creation. God has to be in everything God creates, in me, in the people with ALS, and in all of nature around us. Could we say that God is in creation rather than over and above creation; that God *inter-is* rather than is or is not?

---

[3]Amyotrophic lateral sclerosis.

[4]A bodhisattva is a being with certain qualities that have been developed to a high degree. These qualities include compassion, understanding, respect, and many others. Avalokiteśvara is the bodhisattva who represents the qualities of compassion and listening deeply.

God is a word, a number of phonemes. *Champignon* is a French word. Someone who knows French and English will appreciate that the same reality lies behind the word *mushroom* as lies behind the word *champignon*. However, you could say that the French person's experience of *champignon* is different from the English person's experience of mushroom. In France, they may eat mushrooms differently, they may go looking for different kinds of mushrooms, and so on. Nevertheless, we can assume broadly that when a French person says *champignon* he is referring to the same object as when an English person says mushroom.

In Buddhism, we talk about nirvana. The word originally means extinguishing the fire. We do not feel at ease because there is always some underlying anxiety, fear, or craving. We never feel secure, but it is possible to end the feelings of fear and insecurity, and then the flames are put out and we can feel at ease in the world in which we live. We say that nirvana is neither being nor nonbeing, because it is always available to us though we are not always available to it. When we are in touch with nirvana, we no longer feel that there is a separate self. Everything is intertwined in a marvelous way. So we could say that the words *nirvana* and *God* are different but are pointing to the same human experience.

The teachings on nirvana and God are not intellectual morsels of food for us to enjoy. They are concrete teachings that we can practice in our daily lives. They help us transform emotions such as jealousy, anger, and infatuation. As far as jealousy is concerned, I learn to see myself in the person who makes me jealous and to see that person in me. There was a time when my father was very angry with me. It was an outburst of anger, coming from so much grief and frustration. I was breathing consciously and I recognized that when my father was angry with me, he was angry with himself. I suddenly felt much compassion for him, and at that moment his anger stopped and he apologized. Teachings on God and nirvana help us end the many ideas we have and that we become imprisoned in. An idea about God will not help us when we are on our death-beds. We need to have experienced God in our daily lives in order to be able to continue to experience and be in touch with God as we die. All beliefs in terms of words and ideas will have to cease as we die. All we can do is experience the love of God and the depth of emptiness. Therefore, in our daily lives we need to practice experiencing these things by experiencing interbeing and the oneness of the subject and object of perception.

22

The Greek New Testament

Jesus did not speak in Greek. We do not have certain evidence that his teachings were written down in the language he spoke, but the New Testament we use in the West is translated from Greek. Every time we translate something from one language to another, we lose something of the original meaning. Normally we read the Bible in our native language, so it has been translated at least twice: once from either spoken or written Aramaic into Greek and then again from Greek into English or French, etc. The farthest back I can go when reading the New Testament is to the Greek, but I always have to remind myself not to be too sure that the Greek is a true rendering. The Syriac New Testament, *Peshitta*, differs from the Greek in some instances, and it sometimes makes more sense.[1] Some

---

[1]At Luke 14:26 the word *hate* in the Greek testament is put aside in the Peshitta. In the Greek version of Matthew, the word *camel* (as in, it is easier for a camel to get through the eye of a needle) is *rope* in the Peshitta.

maintain it was translated from the Greek, others that it is older than the Greek.

I often thought when reciting the Lord's Prayer that it was strange that we should be asking God to give us bread every day. Sandwiched between expressing our aspiration to do the will of God and a petition for forgiveness for our wrongdoings in accord with how we forgive others who have wronged us, it seems to be out of context to ask for bread to eat every day. Think about the words of Jesus in Matthew 6:32–33: "So do not worry, saying, 'What shall we eat?' or 'What shall we drink?' or 'What shall we wear?' For the pagans run after all these things, and your heavenly Father knows that you need them. But seek first his kingdom and his righteousness, and all these things will be given to you as well." Or consider John 6:26: "Do not work for the food that spoils, but for food that endures to eternal life." The word *daily* is how St. Jerome translated *epiousion* from Greek into Latin (*cotidianum*) in one place, but in another he changed the translation to *supersubstantialem* (which could mean spiritual). Maybe we should translate asking for our spiritual food using the other translation that St. Jerome provides for *epiousion* (*supersubstantialem*). The Syriac version is translated as needful, what we need in order to be able to live.

If we look at the French translation of *cotidianum*, *"Donnez-nous aujourd'hui notre pain de ce jour,"* it also has meaning. We specifically ask for food just for today, and when we eat, we do not want to think about what we are going to eat tomorrow. On a personal level, for my daily practice to be concrete, the interpretation I prefer is "Give us today our bread of today." When I say these words as I eat, I immediately remember to come back to the present moment and just eat my bread of today, that is, the bread that I have here in front of me. This

interpretation stops my mind from wandering into the future as I eat. I am not thinking about what I shall have to eat tomorrow, what I shall eat for the next meal, or even the next mouthful. For me, this interpretation is completely in accord with what Jesus teaches in Matthew chapter 6. The word used in the Peshitta is also meaningful. It is the word *needful*, meaning necessary. If we use this word, we can contemplate on whether we eat what we need to live a happy and healthy life or do we live to eat and eat what we do not need. Eating simply and with moderation could be what is encouraged by the Syriac version.

Another word in Greek is *engiken*, the verb meaning to be near. It is a translation of the Semitic root *karav* meaning to be near. So, it is not the best translation to say the Kingdom of Heaven is at hand, which makes us think it will come soon in the future. It would be better to say the Kingdom of Heaven is very close to you if you know how to be available to it. Once Thay said to a Catholic nun, "The Kingdom of Heaven is now or never." She understood and smiled.

This raises the question of our daily and ultimate concerns. In the beginning we can see clearly that there are these two dimensions to our lives. Our daily concerns are necessary because we need to eat, sleep, take care of our health, and that of others. Even in the monastery we cannot entirely devote ourselves to our ultimate concern. St. Benedict has taught that to work is to pray. It is not practical, except in rare cases, to sit in meditation or to engage in prayer and contemplation in the chapel all day. We all need times of retreat when we can address our ultimate concerns in meditation or contemplation. We can reserve a certain time every day in our busy lives for meditation or contemplation. If the only time we address our ultimate concerns is an annual retreat or daily hour of meditation, it is like trying to cook potatoes by boiling them a few seconds then taking them off the heat and some hours later boiling them a few more seconds. They will never cook. This is where mindfulness is necessary. It enables us to bring into every moment of our daily lives an attitude that fosters awareness—even though while we are cooking, we can only observe the nature of the vegetables we are cooking, this is not divorced from our ultimate concern of seeing the true nature of things. To live our lives skillfully, we need to bring our everyday concerns and our ultimate concerns as close together as possible.

If you have a difficult relationship in your life, the way to address it is not to sweep it under the carpet by spending your time in metaphysical speculation on the nature of phenomena or God. The difficulty needs your acceptance, attention, and care.[2] The difficulties you encounter in your daily life are a reminder to stay in the historical dimension in order to deal with them.

[2]See Chapter 6.

23

Thҽ Ethics of Mindfulnҽss

∾

As a child I was always moved when I heard the words in Psalm 119, verse 34, "Give me understanding and I will observe your Law and keep it wholeheartedly."

Verse 35: "Guide me in the way of your Commandments for my delight is there."

The human species needs ethical guidelines to follow; otherwise we can destroy ourselves and other species. However, commandments imposed from the outside cannot bring us the delight that is expressed in verse 35. We feel under a constraint, and we obey out of a sense of duty or fear. That is why the basis needs to be understanding—a deep understanding that we can say "is of God." When we understand from our own experience that the reason for following this or that ethical guideline is for the prevention of our own suffering and that of others and the increase of universal happiness, we have great delight in following it. Verse 35 goes further: "I shall live in freedom because I have observed your precepts." Ethical guidelines are to be seen as much more than constraints. In the beginning, our mind is like a wild horse and may need to be constrained, but that is only for the time being. As soon as possible, we need to follow ethical guidelines out of our own understanding. To be able to drink alcohol is not freedom. In fact, the addiction to alcohol and drugs is one of the greatest bondages. To be able to indulge in pornography or virtual sex on the Internet is not freedom. It is a bondage that takes all real love out of our lives. The energies of craving and sexual desire create this bondage and a lot of suffering for ourselves and our loved ones. Deeply ingrained habit energies and instincts can prevent us from seeing clearly our way ahead. This is why as a human species we need ethical guidelines.

In 1993, a World Parliament of Religions was held in Chicago so that world religious leaders could come to some agreement about a common way ahead for all religions in the field of ethics. At the end of the session, they published a declaration with four directives on which they could all agree. They described these directives as *four broad, ancient guidelines for human behavior, which are found in most of the religions of the world.*

1. Commitment to a culture of nonviolence and respect for life. The Judeo–Christian commandment not to kill is cited, and an exhortation to practice noninjury and nonviolence is added.

2. Commitment to a culture of solidarity and a just economic order. The Judeo–Christian commandment not to steal is cited, and an exhortation to commit to do something to relieve poverty in the world is added.

3. Commitment to a culture of tolerance and a life of truthfulness. The Judeo–Christian commandment not to lie is cited, and an exhortation not to preach fanaticism and intolerance is added.

4. Commitment to a culture of equal rights and partnership between men and women. The Judeo–Christian commandment not to commit sexual immorality is cited, and the injunction not to degrade others to mere sexual objects is added as well as the injunction to see that human fulfillment is not identical with sexual pleasure.[1]

In Buddhist terms, what is called Right Mindfulness and Ethics are one and the same thing. You cannot take

---

[1] A paraphrased citation from "Toward a Global Ethic" of the World Parliament of Religions, Chicago 1993.

ethics out of mindfulness (or, if you do, it becomes wrong mindfulness), and you cannot take mindfulness out of ethics. When we are aware of what we are doing and aware of the consequences of our actions, that is mindfulness, and if we are aware that what we are doing will cause ourselves and others to suffer, we no longer want to do that thing.

If we look deeply, we see that good and evil are relative. As long as there is good there will be evil and vice versa. In the same way, as long as there is left, there will be right and vice versa. This nondualistic way of thinking is also present in Christianity. We see it in the Ascetical Discourses of Isaiah of Scetis. There is a saying that "f the devils leave me, the angels will too." It is not necessary for good and evil to fight each other. Good embraces evil with love so that evil can be transformed, just as the lotus roots embrace the mud in order to produce flowers. Ethics grows out of this nonduality. It is not blindly following rules but takes into consideration the circumstances that are producing the suffering and the ways that can alleviate the suffering. Sex, for example, is not unethical in itself. It is unethical when it causes suffering. Killing almost always causes great suffering to the perpetrator and the victim, but occasionally there may be circumstances where killing will alleviate suffering. So, it is told in one of the traditional legends that one time the

Bodhisattva[2] was on a boat with many other passengers. One of the passengers was a mass murderer wanting to kill all the other passengers, so the Bodhisattva killed that one murderer. After that, the Bodhisattva had to suffer the consequences of this violent act and spend some time in hell, but he was ready to do that. This is just a story, but it illustrates that in ethics, we are not caught by rules. In ethics, it is understanding and compassion that lead the way.

Recently some Jewish rabbis have been inspired to rewrite the Ten Commandments in the spirit of ethics being based on mindfulness of suffering. The Tenth Commandment on not coveting, for instance, becomes the Tenth Commitment:

> Aware of the suffering caused by excessive consumption of the world's resources, I vow to rejoice in what I have and to live a life of ethical consumption, governed by a recognition that the world's resources are already strained and by a desire to promote ecological sustainability and material modesty; to see the success of others as an inspiration rather than as detracting from my own sufficiency and to cultivate in myself and others the sense that

---

[2] Buddha in a previous lifetime.

I have enough and that I am enough and that there
is enough for everyone.[3]

The first phrase of this new version begins with "Aware
of the suffering," which means the reason we keep these
commandments or commitments is because we have
understood that we reduce suffering by doing so—not
out of blind faith or because it is imposed upon us by
someone else.

The World Parliament of Religions in 1993 came to
the conclusion that there were ethical principles that all
the members present could agree on, but it needs much
more time and effort to be able to practice them together
as a global community.

We pray that together with others we shall be able to
make progress toward a global ethic.

---

[3]"The Ten Commitments" by Rabbi Richard Lerner, March 2011,
www.tikkun.org/ten-commitments. Based on the Ten Principles for Living
a Life of Integrity by Rabbi Rami Shapiro.

24

Monasticism in the Twenty-First Century

☙

In the gospels, Jesus is reported to have said, "Foxes have holes and the birds of the air have nests, but the son of man has nowhere to lay his head" (Matthew 8:20; Luke 9:58). He was replying to a disciple who wanted to follow him, as if to say, if you want to follow me, you have to give up everything right away. The idea of monasticism is the idea of letting go of material luxuries, practicing celibacy, and living in obedience to your abbot or to your elders or to the decisions made by consensus in your community. These principles are in opposition to many tendencies we have seen in the human race in the past centuries, and so monasticism has either become corrupt or has almost died out. There is always a danger of corruption in the monastic orders, and that is why St. Benedict, St. Augustine, and the Buddha Sakyamuni, to name a few, have established codes of discipline for monks and nuns.

In 1986, I requested Thay to ordain me as a Buddhist nun. His reply was that the West was not ready for monasticism, and if I wanted to be ordained, I should go to Asia. Two years later, Thay agreed to ordain two other women and myself as Buddhist nuns to practice in Europe.

Recently in the United Kingdom there has been a rise in the number of young women (in their twenties and thirties) asking to join the Catholic monastic orders. When asked why, one of them replied, "In order to have freedom: the freedom to devote my life to what is most meaningful: serving God and humanity. Being tied to a job and a family can deprive one of this freedom. It is also to be free of the traps of sex and power." When asked about the vow of chastity, the young novice replied that it is like pruning a tree. You cut away certain branches in order for the tree to be able to send all its sap into the remaining branches. Your energy is put into service rather than raising a family.

We could define monasticism as communal living under the strictures of chastity, poverty, and obedience. The interpretation of poverty and obedience can differ from community to community, but the principle of poverty is to live simply without material luxuries, content with a little less than enough. Obedience can be to the elders of the community, the abbot, abbess, bishop (in the Catholic tradition), or to the consensus of the fully ordained monks or nuns in the community (in the Buddhist tradition).

It might be possible in the future to establish monastic communities in different regions of each country where monks and nuns of different traditions could be based. There would be activities and services the monastic members of the different traditions could perform together and ones they could perform as their separate traditions. These communities could serve as spiritual oases and places of refuge for people of different faiths. It would be a step toward a global ethic and spirituality.

In French, when talking about a monastic community, we can refer to *la fraternité* (*sororité*) and in English to the brotherhood (sisterhood). These words also mean a feeling of kinship with our fellow practitioners. We leave our blood family and join a spiritual family. We organize our community as a family: the mother superior, the father superior, the brothers, the sisters. The way in which we relate to each other is very important. We do not carry on our meditation or practice of prayer in isolation from the rest of our family. We have time to be there for each other; to listen to each other's difficulties and offer support. We take care of the members of our community who are sick. We look on each member of our sisterhood as we would on our blood sister or daughter.

When I was living in our Buddhist monastery in Vermont, we had a Benedictine Priory nearby. The monks there knew about our tradition and Thay (one of them had put one of Thay's poems to music), and we would biannually have days of practice together: one in our monastery and one in their priory. These were truly days of practice, joining the chanting of the liturgy or practicing walking meditation, sitting in a circle and sharing about our practice, eating a meal together.

I enjoyed very much the sessions of sharing. The monks observe the practice of nongyrovague (not going from one monastery to another) or stability—staying always in the same monastery. Some of the brothers had been together for four decades. I observed how they interacted with each other. There was a natural flow of energy between them because they had become like different parts of the same body. When they shared in a discussion, each sharing would flow along as a continuation of what the previous brother had said. This feeling of being one body is something we all aspire to as monks and nuns. It is the kind of brotherhood and sisterhood that we need so much in our own time.

We are monks and nuns, and we are human beings. Some of us come from families with many difficulties, and we can bring those difficulties into our spiritual family. We need ways to be able to reestablish communication when we become angry with someone. There is also the matter of becoming too close or attached to one member of the community, which needs to be dealt with sometimes. In our own time, we need very clear disciplines as far as sex is concerned. A monastic code that is very clear on appropriate comportment and that is read and studied regularly is very beneficial. Sexual energy is not something that disappears when we are ordained as a monk or a nun, nor can we cut it off by repression or denial. However, many of us can handle it and prevent it becoming too strong. Exercise, playing sports for the young, help us handle this energy. We also need the right kind of diet. A diet heavy in protein and eating late at night produces extra energy that we do not need.

Then there is the food that we consume with our eyes and ears. This is a real threat to the practice of celibacy in our own times. Those who practice chastity need to protect themselves from certain websites, films, and other media that arouse sexual energy. The food of our volition and deep aspirations also plays an important role. Our vows to be in communion with God and to help all beings to suffer less can give us a lot of energy that can keep our sexual energy in balance. How we consume not only edible food but the food that comes through our eyes and ears and the food that springs from our deep aspirations is very important for our monastic lives. Our happiness as a monk or a nun is very important. If we are fulfilled in our vocations and have a good rapport with our fellow monks or nuns, our vocations will remain the most important thing to us. If we do not have good communication with our monastic brothers or sisters and do not find happiness in our service and practice, we look for fulfillment in other ways.

Does the twenty-first century need the monastic orders? Of course, as a nun I would say it does. Monks and nuns are a reminder of the presence of the spiritual dimension. This is why I delight in wearing the monastic garb. It is not to cut me off from others; rather, it is to remind others that there is a spiritual dimension. The shaved head, the tonsure, the headscarf, or the veil do not make the monk or nun, nor do the robes. However, while the robes or the hairstyle remind others of the spiritual dimension, they are a constant reminder to the bearer of them to represent authentically from the inside what they are wearing on the outside. Every time we put on our long robes, we remember to adorn ourselves with the practice of the monastic discipline and mindfulness, the decorum of a monk or nun, in order to be able to adorn the world with the spiritual dimension.

While monks and nuns do not have their own families, they have a responsibility to care for the young ones. Children and teenagers who come to our monastery feel very at ease in the presence of monks and nuns. I have heard children say that they feel completely safe with the monks or nuns. I remember myself as a child feeling more at ease with the nuns who taught me than I did with the lay teachers. The nuns were always there. They did not go home at the end of the school day. They had time for us in the evening and on the weekends. No doubt some of them were better-tempered than others, but on the whole, I felt very safe.

25

Religion and Science

⌀

Once when I gave a talk at Heidelberg University to an animal rights group, I mentioned some neuroscience findings. One student was pleasantly surprised. He had always understood that people who were primarily religious were averse to neuroscience because it sought to prove that spiritual devotion comes from a certain part of our brain and has nothing to do with a spiritual realm that is real outside of our consciousness. Actually, the findings of neuroscience can be very helpful for our spiritual practice. When we understand some of the workings of our brains, we are better able to transform or develop our own brains in the direction that our spiritual lives demand.

Public interest in this subject has been aroused by the Dalai Lama's enthusiasm for science. He writes, "If scientific analysis were conclusively to demonstrate certain claims in Buddhism to be false, then we must accept the findings of science and abandon those claims."[1] Similarly Thay has written and spoken on this subject and has maintained a lively interest in scientific matters. We are encouraged as spiritual teachers to be aware of the latest findings of science that are made available to the general public, so that our teachings can be relevant to the young people and our own time.

Many of us, including scientists, would like a spiritual path that can go hand in hand with science. A mystic or a yogi practices prayer or meditation in order to be in touch with the nature of God and the nature of creation. We resist the temptation to close our eyes before scientific evidence because we are afraid it will diminish our faith in our spiritual path. Our path of spiritual practice can be broad enough to embrace science. As practitioners of religion we can also say, "Discoveries by yogis can be verified by science and scientists should accept the truth of those discoveries if they are not able to disprove them."[2] For example, we could say that the efficacy of prayer is something demonstrable to a certain extent by science. We pray for someone far from us and their situation improves at the very time we make the prayer, although they do not know that we are praying for them. Science

---

[1] Dalai Lama XIV, *The Universe in a Single Atom: The Convergence of Science and Spirituality* (New York: Morgan Road Books, 2005), 3.

[2] Thich Nhat Hanh in "Letter to a Young Scientist" (2012).

can demonstrate the nonlocal in the world of particles. It has yet to be demonstrated in terms of the macroscopic world. Some scientists have shown that the molecular structure of water that has been prayed over differs from that of water that has been ignored. This discovery could remain purely theoretical. On the other hand, there are scientists who derive from this discovery the knowledge that we need to speak kindly to our children and not ignore them, because our children are at least 70 percent water.

There are many scientists who practice to see God as they do scientific research. This practice is not a hindrance to their openness. It is not a superstition. For instance, an astrophysicist while looking into the composition of the material that makes the stars will see that the same material is to be found in the atoms in a human being. This observation puts us in touch with our interbeing nature with everything in the universe. Observing the vastness of the galaxies and the cosmos is not something that diminishes the feeling of divine presence. It fills us with wonder and awe. A scientist examining a human heart can see God in the workings of the heart and still write a scholarly paper on the nature of the workings of the heart.

Thanks to advances in science and to the ancient wisdom handed down by different spiritual traditions, we have a chance in the twenty-first century to remove many dichotomies that have plagued the human brain for a very long time. One of these dichotomies is that between matter and spirit. Recently I watched a film where a Russian Orthodox priest blessed water with a crucifix. He held the golden cross in his hands and moved it back and forth in a large container of water. He was clearly heedful of every movement he made. His mind was completely involved with what his body was doing. We do not have to be Zen masters in order to be able to see if someone is completely involved in what he is doing or not. After that, some scientists took the water and looked at it under the microscope. The molecular structure was completely different from that of water just taken from the tap. It had a molecular structure that looked like a magnified snowflake or a crystal. The molecules of the tap water were haphazardly joined together.

When we recognize how our spirits interact with material elements, we are very mindful of our mental attitudes, of what we are thinking and of how we are relating to earth, water, fire, and air.

Science can help demonstrate the oneness of the subjective and objective world, of consciousness and the object of consciousness. This is something that has been realized by yogis and mystics for a very long time. The consciousness and the object of consciousness arise together. Scientists have seen that as soon as they begin to observe a particle, it changes its nature, and from that point of view, there is no objective reality to be observed. Rather than talk about an observer, we have to talk about a participator. Neuroscience says that we see with our brain and not with our eyes. If a tree falls in the forest and no one is there, it does not make a sound. The sound arises from the cortex of the brain.

There is a story about St. Francis of Assisi, which I have

heard from Thay and which I like very much. In the middle of winter, the saint was walking in nature and saw an almond tree. He spoke to it: "Brother Almond Tree, speak to me of God." The almond tree responded by bursting into flower.

As far as particle physicists are concerned, the observer cannot be separated from the observed; as soon as we begin to observe a particle, it changes its nature. Normally we do not observe such an event in the macroscopic world. If we perceive a macroscopic object, we are not aware that it changes because of our perceiving it. Actually, if we look at it for a minute, it will have changed because of the fact of impermanence, but we are not aware of that change either. Someone who has realized her oneness with the object of her perception can perceive the macroscopic object in a way that most of us who have not realized the oneness of our consciousness with the object of perception cannot. The perception of oneness with the object begins with the perception of interbeing.

Once I was asked to lead a day of mindfulness for Catholic nuns. I wanted to talk about creation, and I was not sure whether I would upset the nuns. In the light of modern science, we cannot take literally what we read in the Book of Genesis. In the 1960s with the discovery by biologists of endosymbiosis, we have to look deeply into evolution again. It seems that beginning more than 2 billion years ago and continuing until 800 million years ago, there was a process whereby bacteria made their way into prokaryotic cells carrying with them their own DNA. Our human body could not function without the mitochondria, which were originally bacteria that made their way into animal cells. Darwin was the first to shake the creation story, and now the discoveries of Darwin have themselves been modified by discoveries made in the twentieth century. No doubt, microbiologists will continue to discover things that will modify our understanding of the evolution of life.

As you sit in meditation and become aware of your breathing, you realize that without the microbes in the respiratory system and without the mitochondria in your cells the breathing could not take place. This is a moment when you feel: there is no I breathing. The breathing is manifesting as a wonderful part of life. It is a miracle to be part of this process called life. As a meditator you are a kind of scientist, looking deeply into the nature of your body and mind. No dogma can stand in the way of this deep looking. The nuns were, at least as they expressed with me, very happy to hear that.

It is said in Christianity that we humans are made in the image of God. For me, this means that we have the capacity to represent all that God is: understanding, love—but we also have the capacity to represent all that is not God—hatred, violence, ignorance. When we understand the science of evolution, we can accept that the human species is not perfect, is not the highest species. We humans are just one of the many animal species and we are still evolving and we need to evolve in a direction of understanding and love.

26

Brotherhood and Sisterhood

☙

In Psalm 133 we read, "How good, how delightful it is to live as brothers all together." In spite of this, some of us prefer to live alone. Alone we feel that we can do what we want without inconveniencing others. Others are very afraid of loneliness. Many would like to have a mixture of time to be alone and time to be in the company of others. We do not enter a community so much out of fear of being alone, but rather because we see how rich life in a community can be. No two human beings are exactly alike. No two brains are exactly alike. Everyone has strengths and weaknesses. One may be a good cook, another a not-so-good cook, but a wonderful arranger of flowers. One can have a green thumb and another be an eloquent speaker or writer. The richness is in our being able to pool our talents.

A good abbot, abbess, or community leader is someone who is able to spot the talents in each of the brothers and sisters and put them to good use. Sometimes someone may not see her own strengths. Others in the community can see them and encourage that person to develop them. If we live on our own, we have no one to help us develop. My mother had a special container that she used for washing potatoes. She would turn the handle and the potatoes would rub up against each other, causing the mud to fall off. Living in community we rub up against each other. It is not always so comfortable to be reminded of our shortcomings, but it is always a wonderful opportunity to develop humility and transform some less fortunate characteristics we may have.

27

Parables

꽃

It is said that the emperor Aśoka sent Buddhist missionaries to Greece in the mid-third century BCE. The conquests of the Greek emperor Alexander and the Roman Empire with its trade routes also contributed to links between Indian and Christian and Judaic thought. It is not surprising that there is a similarity between a parable in the Lotus Sutra[1] and the story of the prodigal son (Luke 15:11–32) as well as between the Sutra on Water, as an example,[2] and the story of the Samaritan going from Jerusalem to Jericho (Luke 10:25–37). There has been some sort of interbeing between Buddhism and Christianity, although we cannot know exactly how and when.

When we come together in interfaith gatherings to

---

[1] Chapter 4.
[2] AN 5, 162 and MA 25.

practice and worship, we can contemplate the following parables. From the Christian biblical point of view, the parable of the man on the road from Jerusalem to Jericho is about developing the capacity to see a person who is in need of help as our neighbor, whom we should learn to love as we love ourselves, whatever his creed may be. From the Buddhist sutra point of view, it is about changing our way of looking at the person with whom we are angry. We develop our capacity to look on the person, who seems to us to have no goodness of body, speech, or mind, as someone who is suffering greatly and needs our help, not our blame and punishment.

The gospels, as well as the sutra, recount a parable concerning a runaway son. The fundamental meaning is that we run away from God or run away from the Buddha. We could also say that we run away from that of God within us or that of the Buddha within us. In the case of the biblical prodigal son, it is a matter of living an unwholesome life and then repenting. In the case of the Buddhist sutra, it is a matter of running away from one's father and not feeling worthy of receiving one's rightful inheritance.

This feeling of unworthiness, whether it is because we have committed harmful actions or not, is an impediment to our progress on the spiritual path. It can be a complex that prevents us from realizing our full potential. Of course, the complex of arrogance and self-pride is also an obstacle. We need to transform all our complexes, by realizing that we *inter-are* and do not have a separate self.

By combining these two different interpretations of similar parables, our understanding is enriched.

Luke 10:25–37

An expert in the Jewish law asked Jesus how he could have eternal life. Jesus did not answer but asked a question in return:

"What is said about this in the law?"

The expert answered,

"You should love God with all your strength, your heart, and soul and love your neighbor as yourself."

The expert in the law wanted to test Jesus so he asked,

"Who is my neighbor?"

Jesus replied,

"A man was going from Jerusalem to Jericho, when he was attacked by robbers, who stripped him of his clothing and left him half dead by the side of the road. A priest saw him and passed by on the other side. A Levite did the same but a Samaritan bandaged his wounds, took him to the nearest inn, and gave money to the innkeeper to take care of him.

"Of the three who passed by who was the neighbor?"

"The one who took care of him."
Jesus said,
"Go and do the same."

Anguttara Nikaya 5, 162 and Madhyamaka Agama 25

Śāriputra, a senior disciple of the Buddha, was teaching his fellow monks what to do when you become angry with someone. He said, "Suppose a man is going on a journey and on the road he falls sick. The village he left is far behind and the next village is far ahead. He is alone, without resource and feels that he is going to die. Then someone comes along who sees this man's situation. He brings the sick man to the next village and makes sure he has food, medicine, and all he needs to get well. In this way the man's life is saved.

"When you are angry with someone because there is no purity in his actions of body, speech, and mind, contemplate on that person to see that he is like someone who is very sick and needs your help in order not to fall into realms of great suffering."

Luke 15:11ff.

People were criticizing Jesus for sitting with tax collectors and others who were considered to be of depraved moral character. He spoke a number of parables about the joy in heaven when someone who has done wrong repents of his wrongdoing.

"A man has two sons. He gives them their inheritance. The younger son takes his share and goes to live in a far-off place where he squanders it on high living. Then there is a famine in that land and he has no more money. He has to work as a hired laborer taking care of pigs. He is so hungry he longs to eat the food he is feeding the pigs. Then he thinks to himself,

'In my father's house they have more than enough to eat. Why do I not go home to my father and repent and ask him to let me be a hired worker?' "

So he goes back to his father's house. His father sees him coming in the distance and full of love runs out to meet his son. The son says,

"Father, I have sinned against heaven and against you and am no more worthy to be called your son. Let me be one of your hired servants." The father says to his servants,

"Put a robe on him and sandals on his feet and kill the fatted calf."

The elder son was angry. All these years he had worked for his father but no celebration had been held in his honor.

The father said,

> "Son, we have to celebrate because my son whom we lost has come home. You are always with me and all I have is yours."

Jesus said,

> "There is more joy in heaven over one sinner who repents than over ninety-nine who have not sinned."

Lotus Sutra, chapter 4

A young man runs away from home, seduced by foolish friends, in order to make his living in a distant land. His father goes from place to place looking for him and at the same time becomes very rich. The son becomes poorer and poorer. In search of a living, the son also goes from place to place. Eventually father and son end up in the same town. The father is sitting in the entrance to his mansion distributing alms to the poor. The son wants to receive alms but feels that the place is too magnificent and doubts it will be good to stay around. The father has recognized his son and sends attendants to bring the son to him, but the son refuses to come. He is afraid of what they might do to him. So, the father thinks of a ruse. He has his attendants employ the son to do the work of clearing a pile of excrement in his grounds. Thus, father and son can be near each other, even though the son has no idea that this is his father. The father gradually approaches the son and expresses his approval for his son's character and work. After many years, the son is able to accept that this is his father and receive his inheritance.

28

Jesus Christ and Sakyamuni Buddha as Brothers

Thay wrote a book with the title of this chapter as a subtitle[1] and inspired by that, an artist painted Christ and Buddha standing alongside each other as brothers. The painting was on our altar in Plum Village for some time.

Contemplating the lives of Christ and Buddha, we see that both were revolutionaries in the spiritual domain who wanted to renew the spiritual traditions of their time. Both Christ and Buddha were rooted in spiritual traditions that had lost some of the spiritual dynamic. In the Christian scriptures, Jesus Christ refers to the new

---

[1] Thich Nhat Hanh, *Going Home: Jesus and Buddha as Brothers* (New York: Riverhead Books, 1999).

covenant, which means a new way for humankind to relate to God. There were social injustice and corruption in the hierarchy. In Palestinian society there were divisions between the different Hebrew tribes and Jewish sects and racial discrimination. There were religious practices, rites, rituals, and laws, which had become an outer form without a spiritual content. In Indian society in the fifth and sixth centuries BCE, society was divided by a cruel caste system that was based on racial discrimination.[2] There were violent struggles for power. There was the practice of animal sacrifice, the brahmin priests were held to be the medium between the people and the deities and wielded too much spiritual power. In India as in Palestine there were movements away from the status quo. There were the Sramanas who practiced asceticism and meditating in the forest. The Upanishads were an important step forward because they held that everyone has the capacity to be in touch with Brahma, the Supreme, by their own meditation, not needing the intervention of the priestly caste. In Palestine there were the Essenes from the second century BCE. In India different sects had their dogma, their theories about the nature of the universe, and were in constant dispute with each other.

The community of the Buddha was free from the

---

[2]The Sanskrit word for caste is *varna*, which means color.

caste system; a barber was an elder brother to princes. Jesus wanted to go back to the pure source of spirituality, free from meaningless outer rules and rites. The Buddha was not a Buddhist, and Jesus was not a Christian. Both were open to teach and help anyone who came to them whatever their race or creed.

Jesus and Buddha have descendants who continue to keep Christianity and Buddhism from becoming fossilized in outer forms that can become superstition. Martin Luther King Jr. was brave to undertake nonviolent resistance for the human rights of Black people, to use his voice to shake Christians out of complacency with a cruel system. "If today's church does not recapture the sacrificial spirit of the early church, it will lose its authenticity, forfeit the loyalty of millions, and be dismissed as an irrelevant social club with no meaning for the twentieth century."[3] Thich Nhat Hanh struggled against the Buddhist hierarchy to renew Buddhism and against political forces to bring peace to Vietnam. The causes and conditions were right for the two of them to come together in the 1960s to strengthen each other's resolve to build the *beloved community.*

---

[3]"Letter from a Birmingham Jail."

Concluding Exercise

∽

To conclude, following is an exercise to help us practice in difficult and not so difficult moments. It is suitable for double-belongers and single-belongers, and helps us to see that Christianity and Buddhism are different rivers going down to the same ocean.

This exercise removes two kinds of dualism: the dualism that says that Christianity is outside of Buddhism and the dualism that says that Jesus (or Buddha) is outside of me.

Thay taught me this exercise in a Buddhist context. Since then, I have also practiced it in a Christian context.

There are times when I have felt I am going to fall into a depression or despair. A darkness envelops my mind. I know that I do not want to go down that path into an abyss, so I send an SOS message to Jesus Christ or the Buddha. I know that Jesus and the Buddha are in every cell of my body because I have been their student and their disciple, and they have transmitted so many wonderful things to me. Sometimes it is easier for me to send the message to Jesus because my child's mind was infused with images and feelings of Jesus as was the mind of my genetic ancestors. That is just a preference from my upbringing and culture. We should know what is most accessible from our unconscious to call up into our conscious mind.

I say, "Jesus, breathe!" and I just let Jesus breathe, I feel I do not have to do anything else. After some breaths I notice that Jesus is breathing with my lungs. I say to myself, "Jesus is breathing." The breath of Jesus is entering every cell of my body and I enjoy the feeling. I then notice the presence of Jesus by means of the breathing, in the breathing. The reason I know Jesus is present is because that is the kind of breath that Jesus would make. So Jesus is the breathing. I also recognize that, as I concentrate on breathing, I am the breathing, and I am not separate from Jesus. At that moment I am the breather and Jesus is the breather and the breather is not separate from the breathing.

So, the next part of the exercise is to see that there is only breathing. You could say there is only the breath of God or the breath of the Holy Spirit. There is only that and there is no one breathing.

I can dwell peacefully in that breathing, and I notice there is peace while breathing. Finally I notice that the breathing is the peace and the peace is the breathing. It is no longer necessary to separate peace from breathing and breathing from peace.

If you like you can add the position of your body to this exercise. While practicing, your body will either be sitting, lying, or walking. You ask Jesus to lie, sit, or walk with your body. Jesus walks very gently and mindfully and lies very relaxed, sits very upright so the blood can flow well.

Here is a synopsis of the exercise:

Jesus, breathe! Jesus, walk!

Jesus is breathing. I enjoy the breathing. Jesus is walking. I enjoy the walking.

Jesus *is* the breathing. I am the breathing. Jesus *is* the walking. I am the walking.

There is only breathing. There is no one breathing. There is only walking. There is no one walking.

Peace while breathing. Joy while walking.

Peace is the breathing. Joy is the walking.

If you want you can replace "Jesus" with "Buddha."